A Family Place

A Family Place

A Man Returns to the Center of His Life

Charles Gaines

THE ATLANTIC MONTHLY PRESS
NEW YORK
·

FIRST EDITION

Library of Congress Cataloging-in-Publication Data

Gaines, Charles, 1942–

A family place: a man returns to the center of his life / Charles
Gaines.—1st ed.

ISBN 0-87113-560-4

I. Gaines, Charles, 1942–   —Homes and haunts—Nova Scotia.

2. Novelists, American—20th century—Biography. 3. Nova Scotia—

Social life and customs.   I. Title.

PS3557.A353Z467   1994   813'.54—dc20   93-28569

Design by Laura Hough

The Atlantic Monthly Press
841 Broadway
New York, NY 10003

FIRST PRINTING

To Patricia

To Latham, Greta, and Shelby

To Hansell Gaines Burke and Margaret Shook Gaines

And to Hestia

ACKNOWLEDGMENTS

I want to thank the residents of East Tracadie, Nova Scotia, for the generosity and kindness with which they met the Gaines family's appearance among them. Particularly, I want to thank Ralph DeCoste for his help in researching the historical part of this book, and for the example and friendship of his family. I also want to thank Dan Green for his determined vision.

"When we build, let us think that we build forever. Let it not be for the present delight nor for present use alone. Let it be such work as our descendants will thank us for; and let us think, as we lay stone on stone, that a time is to come when those stones will be held sacred because our hands have touched them, and that men will say, as they look upon the labor and wrought substance of them, 'See! This our father did for us!' "

—John Ruskin

"There are no events but thoughts and the heart's hard turning, the heart's slow learning where to love and whom."

—Annie Dillard, *Holy the Firm*

I

This is a book about family and finding a place in the world where family is important. Seventeen summers ago, when our three children were still children, my wife, Patricia, and I took them on a two-week driving tour of Nova Scotia. The purpose of that trip was to isolate ourselves from everything but the healing joy of family closeness. Last summer we all returned to Nova Scotia to do the same thing. This time we did it by building a cabin there for ourselves, with our own hands, and by rebuilding with our own hands the family that would occupy it.

For three months before our first tour of Nova Scotia we had lived in Alabama while the movie of my first novel was being filmed there. Up until the modest success of that novel and the invitation to move to Alabama as coscreenwriter for the film adaptation of it, Patricia and I and our kids had lived a quiet, determinedly rural life in New Hampshire. We went to bed early and got up early together to eat breakfast around a wood stove. We skied together, climbed mountains together, cut wood together, and weathered storms together. When Patricia learned from my agent that the movie rights to my novel had been sold, she and the kids strung balloons inside our little rented house on Lake Sunapee and threw me a surprise party. We believed then that we had good reason to celebrate.

But the three months of filming in my hometown of Birmingham opened a Pandora's box for Patricia and me, and it was years before we could close that box again. We told ourselves we had been shut up in the hills paying bills for a long time, and would soon enough go back to that, and that a little fun never hurt anybody. In no time, I went from a one-Pop-Tart-a-day dad whose biggest weekend kick was a canoe float with my kids on the Contoocook River to a high-handed, big-appetite experience chaser—a caricature of the country boy gone Hollywood. And too often the glitter, and the odd, bogus sense of power and prerogative that making a movie gives you—the sense that you are somehow part of an occupying force in a small, backward country—made us feel like someone had walked up out of the blue and painted big, red S's on our chests. For the first time in our married life we decided we could leave the dishes for someone else to wash. We flirted with movie stars playing versions of ourselves—and with losing everything that mattered to us.

When the filming ended it was July and a hundred and ten degrees in Birmingham. Patricia and I were thin, wrung out, and snappish with each other; our daughter Greta, then nine, had had nightmares every night in her basement room; and all of us had felt for the first time the cold stomach knot of dread that comes when a family that is everything to each other first springs a leak and the world starts pouring in.

With its clean glimpses of ocean everywhere, its cool, bracing air, and straight ahead, cheerful people, Nova Scotia was just the clarifying restorative we needed. We drove the breath-taking Cabot Trail on Cape Breton Island and hiked its trails. We ate Scottish oatcakes and played board games beside a fire in a tiny inn on the northeast coast as an Atlantic fog cut us off from everything but each other. We stayed for a few days at a working farm where a Shetland pony, a pig, and a St. Bernard followed the kids around and where mowed fields ran right down to the sea. We played a game called "Mug" in the sea-smelling dusks; we read Hardy Boys mysteries aloud to each other at night; and gradually, over the course of the two weeks we were there, Nova Scotia led us back to health and unity.

Patricia and I returned to the province a couple of times together over the next few years, and I went back a number of times alone to fish and shoot, falling for the place a little more each time, finding it a miracle of abundance and variety. In Nova Scotia you can catch shad in the spring, trout, bass, mackerel, and Atlantic salmon all summer long, and giant bluefin tuna in September and October, when the shooting season opens for woodcock and grouse, snipe, ducks, and geese. Lobster bought right off the boats during the season is less than three dollars a pound. You can dig all the clams and mussels you want on any of dozens of beautiful, unpopulated beaches. The sailing in Saint Georges Bay and in the inland sea called Bras d'Or is some of the best in the world. And you can come around a corner anywhere, anytime in Nova Scotia and be face to face with a visual combination of earth, sky, and sea so important you'd think the whole world depended on it.

Manhattan Island was once a paradise. Wild rosebushes

and vast fields of lupine grew in the Bowery. The East and Hudson rivers teemed with striped bass and salmon. Wild turkeys roosted on Wall Street, and black bear denned through the winters along Park Avenue. Downtown Los Angeles, too, was once a good place to live. On the streets that now belong to killer kids, drug addicts, hookers, and the homeless, the Yang-Na Indians had no trouble gathering all the wild cress, grapes, and cucumbers they wanted. And in the smoggy entertainment warrens of Beverly Hills, Brentwood, and Pacific Palisades, Jesuits once rose early in fields red with foxtail and gold with prickly pear and began their matinals to bird song.

As we know, the modern world has ruined many good places to live. And it continues to chug along, implacable and mindless as a pavement eater, ruining more every day and giving rise in many of us to the dream of some "last, best place"—a last-stand place, as yet unruined, where life is still lived as the person with the dream believes it should be lived: with the right priorities, in the right company (or lack of it), at the right tempo, and in collaboration with the right landscape.

Montana is popular, for good reason, as a last, best place. New Zealand could certainly stake a claim. Alaska, Patagonia, Tasmania, and Costa Rica could, too. For somebody, the last, best place may even be Manhattan, who knows? For Patricia and me, over a period of time, it became Nova Scotia, and two years ago we decided to look there for a piece of property to buy. At the time, that seemed a simple, even offhand, decision. We had no inkling that we would soon look to that property for the same blessing of family reuniting and healing that Nova Scotia had bestowed on us seventeen years before, or that it would be the place where my wife and I would learn how to love each other again. At the time, all Patricia thought we were after in our last, best place was a little piece of land by the sea.

The sea is and always has been Nova Scotia's defining element, and the sea's cool blue light is Nova Scotia's light.

The province is shaped like a giant lobster. Less than four hundred miles long, with a maximum width of one hundred miles, it has some five thousand miles of coastline—on the Atlantic Ocean to the south and east, on the Bay of Fundy and Gulf of Saint Lawrence to the west and north—and at no place in the province is it possible to be more than fifty miles from ocean water. So many of Nova Scotia's people have been lobster and scallop fishermen, clammers, trawlers for haddock, hake, cod, mackerel, and herring, handliners of tuna and swordfish, boat builders, sailors, and driers of Irish moss that the sea is a common language to them, a birthright, and a backyard full of sapphires.

Along with the other Atlantic provinces of New Brunswick, Newfoundland/Labrador, and Prince Edward Island, Nova Scotia is a part of the northernmost extension of the Appalachian Mountains and valleys of the eastern United States: old land. Some of its rock dates back a billion years. It might once have been an island in an ocean called Iapetus, which disappeared some 430 million years ago in a collision between North America and Africa that made Morocco and Cape Breton temporary neighbors until the formation of the Atlantic Ocean separated them again and configured Nova Scotia as it is today. The glaciers of the Pleistocene era formed its countless inland lakes and its deep bays and coves and scoured much of the province of its over-burden of topsoil, which is one of the reasons why only one third of Nova Scotia can now be farmed.

The original inhabitants of Nova Scotia were Algonquian-speaking eastern sub-Arctic Indians known as Mi'kmaq, the ancestors of the modern Micmacs. For over ten thousand years before the first Europeans arrived, this people roamed the province, going where the food was, in extended family groups. Family was the most important element of Mi'kmaq life, and it fully organized the Mi'kmaq society. Power accrued to leaders in proportion to the love and respect tendered them by their families and in accordance with how cohesive and stable those families were.

Extended domestic groups of Nova Scotian Mi'kmaqs would make summer camp together on fish-rich, protected waters such as the Bay of Saint George and flourish there on flounder, eel, striped bass, and sturgeon. Harp, gray, and hooded seals provided them with meat and oil. In winter these groups moved inland, living off beaver, porcupine, bear, muskrat, and moose. The marrow, blood, and meat of the moose were eaten by the Mi'kmaq; its hide was used for clothing and snowshoe thongs; its brain for tanning skins; its bladder was filled up with seal oil; its horns were made into tools; its tendons became thread for sewing; its hair was embroidered; its dew claws made into rattles; its shinbones carved into dice; and its hooves were used as a medicine for epilepsy.

This original Nova Scotian was a family man who could make do.

Nova Scotia was first visited by Europeans in 1497 when John Cabot sailed his little ship, *Matthew*, into a bay of Cape Breton Island fifty days out of Bristol. Cabot imagined he was in China, the land of the Great Khan. He found no silk or spices in Nova Scotia, but he did discover unimagined treasures on this voyage and a subsequent one, opening up, on the Great Banks off the eastern coast of Nova Scotia and south of Newfoundland, one of the richest fisheries the world has ever known—a fishery that within a few hundred years would make Nova Scotia the richest of Canada's founding provinces and one of the busiest seaports on earth. The fish in these seas, Cabot reported to King Henry VII, were so thick "they sometimes stopped progress of the ship," so numerous that nets were unnecessary, as a boat could just sink stone-weighted baskets and haul up the treasure. Thrilled almost speechless with this place of beauty and bounty that he had found by accident, Cabot claimed all of Nova Scotia for his king, making it Britain's first colony in the New World.

But it was a Frenchman, the writer, explorer, and bon vivant, Samuel de Champlain, who founded the first settlement in Nova Scotia (and the first permanent European settlement north of Florida) in 1605 at Annapolis Royal, then called Port Royal. Champlain also founded L'Order de Bon Temps, or the Order of Good Cheer. Established to enliven the long winter nights at the outpost of Port Royal, this was the first social club in North America, as well as the first known emergence of the honored Nova Scotian inclination to celebrate during adversity.

By 1621 the French were becoming well established and numerous in what they called Acadia. (The Florentine navigator Verrazano is supposed to have originated this name for Nova Scotia after the Greek region of Arcadia, which epitomized rustic contentment and simplicity.) King James I of Britain was made nervous by this, so he declared Nova Scotia a royal province and gave it to a Scottish poet and courtier named Sir William Alexander to colonize, thus initiating nearly one hundred and fifty years of French-English conflict in the province that was not finally resolved until the surrender of the entire French empire in North America in 1763.

The Acadians, as the original French settlers of Nova Scotia were called, were an industrious, practical people who got along and traded with the Indians, diked low-lying salt marshes to create rich farmland, and became, over the course of the seventeenth century, more and more oblivious to whether it was France or Britain who claimed them as subjects. In 1713 France finally ceded Nova Scotia to Britain. The cession was fine by the Acadians until Britain began pressuring them to sign an "Oath of Allegiance" to take up arms against France if Britain deemed it necessary. Many Acadians refused to do this. Concerned during the French and Indian War that Nova Scotia was harboring a "nest of traitors," in 1755 its British governor deported as many of the Acadians as could be rounded up, starting some of those nearly ten thousand souls on a trail of tears—dramatized in Longfellow's poem, *Evangeline*—that stretched all the way to Louisiana, where their descendants are today called "Cajun," an abbreviation of Acadian.

The British replaced these lost subjects with settlers from northern England and Scotland and colonists from New England. During and after the American Revolution, Nova Scotia became a refuge for thousands more Americans who were loyal to Britain, including many blacks, half the living graduates of Harvard College, and many members of America's commercial, cultural, and social elite who would soon help turn Halifax into one of Canada's most civilized cities. During the eighteenth century Irish, Welsh, and German settlers also moved to Nova Scotia in significant numbers, along with both Protestant and Catholic Scots—all of them looking for a new start in this place Jacques Cartier had called "the finest land it is possible to see."

And finally, after the Treaty of Paris in 1763 ended for good any French political presence in North America, the Acadians were allowed to return, and many of them did come back to join the few who had never left and resume their quiet, independent lives. A part of, but also apart from, what was by now a burgeoning Nova Scotian provincial character, those Acadians who returned were people forced into themselves and their families—into absolute self-reliance and distrust of government—by exile and by the power of their dreams.

Let's look at such a man, a farmer, we'll say, named Barrio. At the time of his expulsion from Acadia, he has lived in the rich Annapolis valley since his birth in 1705: a fifty-year-old man with a wife, three sons, and two daughters. With help from his neighbors and his large extended family, he has diked forty acres of marshland and raised on it wheat and flax. He has a small apple orchard and a vegetable garden. He keeps milk cows and a steer or two for beef, pigs, chickens, sheep, and a pair of oxen. On a pleasant Wednesday evening in September 1755, he is called in to the parish church at Grand Pré with all the other males over ten years old in his community. They are told there by an English colonel named John Winslow that they will have to leave Acadia, leave their land and their homes for good, and that they will be held there in the church until they can be embarked on the ships that will take them away. They are told they will be reunited with their families on the ships, but in many cases they are not. A month later, when Barrio is placed on the sloop *Endeavor,* his wife and daughters are aboard, but not his sons, and he never sees those sons again.

One hundred and eighty Acadians sail south on the *Endeavor.* The forty-two-day journey is a foul misery of too little food and water, overcrowding, and disease. By the time the ship reaches Charleston harbor nearly sixty of the Acadians have died and been thrown into the sea, including Barrio's younger daughter. He and his wife and remaining daughter join with two other families and walk all the way from South Carolina to French-speaking Louisiana where, they are told, other Acadians are going. They arrive in the bayou country in April of 1756.

It is hot. Barrio dreams of the first irises blooming in the bog behind his house, the salt marsh beginning to color, the spring run of shad. For ten years in the eternal muggy summer of the bayou he dreams of the seasons coming and going in Acadia. Acadia is the shape and substance and place of his dreams—and no one has ever dreamed harder. Then, in March of 1764, he learns that some government or another has determined that he can go back home. Barrio is now an old man, his daughter has married a shrimper, and his wife is not well, but he rouses them all and he does that—he goes back home, and all the way north, following the cool blue light of the sea in his mind, his energy freshening like a west wind bringing storm.

These powerful dreamers, these Acadians, were also family men who made do.

Today Nova Scotia has a population of fewer than a million people, a temperate, sea-moderated climate, an interior that is three quarters forest, over one thousand square miles of inland lakes, ponds, and rivers, thriving populations of deer, moose, black bear, coyote, fox, beaver, and mink, and an astonishing profusion of wildflowers. Its geography swings from the tranquil farming and orchard land of the Annapolis valley, which is reminiscent of the American Midwest, to the wild, sea-swept cliffs and coves of Cape Breton Island, which seem to have sprung from some sword-clashing Gaelic myth.

The first hockey game ever played was played in Nova Scotia; the first trans-Atlantic cable transmission was made from Cape Breton, as was the first flight in the British empire. The first Roman Catholic church in North America was in Nova Scotia and the first drama written and staged in North America was produced there. Nova Scotia had the first school in Canada, the first newspaper, the first Protestant church, the first post office, legal trade union, circulating library, and English university.

And finally, in Cape Forchu, Nova Scotia, in 1620, a boy child was born by the blue light of the sea to an Indian woman. The boy was named André Lasnier. His father was Louis Lasnier from Dieppe, France. André Lasnier, a Mi'kmaq Acadian, is believed to be the first child of European extraction born in North America.

On our first trip to the province to look for land Patricia and I flew to Halifax, rented a car, and drove north and east along the Atlantic coastline through postcard-perfect fishing villages with names like Spry Bay, Ecum Secum, and Sheet Harbour. We looked at a foggy, spruce-studded point near Liscomb and at a vast inland wilderness tract near Margaree on Cape Breton Island. A German realtor showed us a small property on Bras d'Or Lake with an active railroad track running through it and told us that his countrymen were buying up all the waterfront land they could find in Nova Scotia. We were fortunate, he said, that somehow the Germans had overlooked this lovely lakeside property with the railroad track. Yes, but it was not what we wanted, we told him; did he have anything else? No, he said: The Germans had bought it all. "You are two years too late," he told us. "Go try New Brunswick."

Nonsense, said Frank Chisholm on our next land-hunting trip to the province. There was plenty of waterfront land in Nova Scotia left to be had at a good price, and he would guarantee that he would find us what we wanted. Patricia had come across Frank's name in a real estate ad. A good-humored, broad-faced Scot, a retired schoolteacher from Antigonish now selling real estate with determination and inspiration, he was exactly what we needed. We were staying in Liscomb, looking along the beautiful, moody eastern shore. We would not be happy down there, Frank told us—it was too cold, too often fog-bound, and too remote from the amenities of a good town. He had some properties up near Antigonish, some fifty miles away on the Gulf of Saint Lawrence side of the province. There was one piece of land in particular, he said, a little larger than what we were looking for maybe, but still we ought to see it.

We left Liscomb with Frank in a chilly fog and drove through the historically restored village of Sherbrooke, followed a lovely, world-renowned salmon river called the Saint Mary's, and broke into full, warm sunlight just short of Antigonish. The little town itself was bright and cheerful and boasted a good Catholic university, a movie theater, a couple of good restaurants and shops, a building supplies store, and an excellent market. Originally settled by Roman Catholic Scots, Bonnie

Prince Charlie's supporters in the Jacobite Rebellion, the town still has a distinct Scottish accent: People walk the streets dressed in kilts, there are often bagpipers playing in front of the bank, and every July Antigonish hosts the largest Highland Games celebration outside of Scotland.

Antigonish is on Saint Georges Bay, a bay of the Gulf of Saint Lawrence bounded by Cape George to the west and by Port Hood on Cape Breton Island to the east. Because of the proximity of the Gulf Stream, the water in the bay is miraculously warm for this part of the world—the warmest water, in fact, anywhere along the Atlantic coast north of North Carolina. Seeing this beautiful, warm, storm-protected body of water from Antigonish for the first time, Patricia and I were immediately smitten. It happened that the property Frank wanted to show us was on the bay just east of Antigonish. "To be honest with you," Frank told us as we began the drive out there, "I think it will be the only property you need to look at."

We drove for about fifteen miles through farming country, then turned off the Trans-Canada highway and followed a back road out along the shore, past a harbor with a small commercial fishing wharf where lobster traps were stacked in piles and five or six lobster boats were docked. Just beyond the wharf we stopped at a trim white farmhouse and went in to meet Walter and Edna Boudreau, the owners of the property.

Edna was seventy and Walter eighty-three. They were second cousins as well as man and wife, direct descendants of one of the Acadian families that had settled this and other small communities along the bay. They both spoke in distinctly French cadences and with an accent that had come from France a long time ago. Walter had a mischievous face and farmer's hands. Edna was a straight, handsome woman with smart, tough eyes and an ironic smile. They had the nearly wordless comfort with each other that comes from years and years of living with the right mate.

Edna made us a cup of coffee and then they both sat looking at us, Walter from his armchair in front of the TV with amused interest, as though we were a new channel he had just tuned in, and Edna, straight-backed in a kitchen chair, with hawkish curiosity. The piece of land we were going to look at had been in their family for over 150 years, she said, first as pastureland, then as a blueberry farm. There was a little shack up there, over a hundred years old, that she remembered separating milk in when she was a child, sleeping in occasionally with her parents as a girl helping with the butter churning, and sorting blueberries in with Walter on summer evenings as a grown woman. There was a long pause in the conversation when Edna finished telling us about the shack. She and Walter studied Patricia and me, smiling and friendly but assessing. "You go look at the land," Edna said finally. "I think maybe you'll like it."

Frank Chisholm drove us from the Boudreau house a few hundred yards over a crest and down to a rocky beach at the end of the road. To our left was the breakwater at the mouth of the harbor, and before us was the full, shining expanse of Saint Georges Bay. Frank pointed right, up the shoreline, to a long, high-cliffed cape jutting into the bay a half mile to the east. "That's it," he said. "Barrio's Head, it's called. There's no road to it anymore, so you'll have to walk."

It was a brilliant day, hot and cloudless, with just enough wind to lift whitecaps off the bay. The water was a deep,

Prussian blue. Patricia and I walked up the beach, turned inland
where it rose into a cliff, crossed a gully, and followed a deer
trail up the cliff and along its brow. At the top we were some
sixty feet above the water at the northern tip of the cape. To the
west the shoreline we had just walked curled behind us into the
graceful harbor with the fishing wharf—Tracadie Harbor, it was
called. To the east of us was another, smaller, very beautiful
harbor with a spit of sand beach forming its northern entrance.
Beyond both harbors were spruce-forested capes separated by
strips of gleaming bay, receding to a smoke-blue horizon of hills
holding the bay on the east and west like two faint arms. It
seemed a plenum, this high, layered outlook of land and water
and bright air—of barns, fishing boats, hay fields, dwellings,
churches; it seemed to contain exactly everything we needed.
What's more, the combination of the brushed green, gently
tenanted land and the wide, blue bay, giving on to open ocean
to the north as if it poured through a chip in a saucer there, was,
Patricia and I knew instantly, a precise physical actualization of
the possibilities we had been looking for up here—the first
visual clue to the shape of the dream we were carrying around.

Behind us the promontory broadened and stretched a full
half mile south to a tree line of spruce. Abandoned some twenty
years ago as pasture for milk cows, then again eight or nine years
ago as a blueberry farm, this high, sea-surrounded meadow, 160
acres of it, had now gone back to a bristly mat of knee- to
chest-high undergrowth and brush. Bayberry, chokecherry, Indian pear, small alder and poplar, blackberry, and spruce; it was
a sociable place, Patricia and I learned as we pushed through
it—full of game trails and signs of rabbit, deer, and coyote.
Wild roses, *rosa floribundi*, were everywhere in bloom. The deli-

cate silver dollar–size pink flowers with their bright yellow hearts were perched in the brush like thousands of migrating pink-and-yellow butterflies, and the air was perfumed with them and with balsam fir.

At the very back of the property, in a small clearing near the tree line, was the weathered little shack Edna had told us about. It was built of hemlock boards and battens, with a spruce-shingle roof, and the old wood had gone a silvery gray. At eight feet by ten feet it was smaller than we had pictured it, but looking out over the neglected fields toward the sea, it was a jaunty, tough little structure with a past, and it gave us our first human point of reference for the land—a place to begin feeling for it and to start making connections.

For the rest of the afternoon Patricia and I wandered over the property, scratching up our legs and arms on brush and getting more and more excited on visions of how we might come to live here—seeing a path to bonfires and clambakes in the sloping hollow of the property's northeast flank where the cliffs ran down to the beach again, seeing a pond in a two-acre marsh full of wild irises, seeing our children on windsurfers in the eastern harbor.

Hours later we went back out to the end of Barrio's Head and stood there in the blue light of an old Mi'kmaq and Acadian sea, the view still stuck in our throats and nothing more to say than, "This is it. This is where we start from now."

2

Here is a story about hunting, food, fatherhood, and home.

It is the 1950s in Birmingham, Alabama. The father in this story lives in a big house that he bought with money he made from working very hard for his wife's family, though he never much liked to work. Working hard for his wife's family and not liking it, along with drinking too much red whiskey, has given him an ulcer, a self-inflicted wound that will almost kill him. He is a big, charming man who has never met a stranger, popular in boardrooms, in private clubs, and on shooting plantations. He is a dedicated civic leader, a great dancer, someone who will fight with his fists and relish it, a devoted husband, a lover of sensation and travel but not of mystery, a bigot, a sentimental realist with a big heart, precise hands, immutable values, a sense of humor, no fear of death, a fine sartorial flair, and no religion beyond hunting and fishing. He knows exactly what he likes and doesn't like, what he believes and doesn't believe. He has absolutely no pretense and, though he is an honors graduate of M.I.T., not the slightest intellectual inclination or urge to ponder his life. He is virile yet high-strung—a saber blade ornately scrolled. And he is a clear sky with one low, dark cloud in it.

Within ten years he will quit drinking overnight and never touch another drop, but for now he is a fierce and secret alcoholic. He hides quart bottles of bourbon from his wife in laundry hampers, his gun closet, the kitchen pantry. And when she is gone he swoops down on them like a hawk on chickens. He makes an effort to hide his drinking, and himself when he is drunk, from his wife and his daughter. But not from his son: He has made his son a partner in the secret.

At the time of this story the son is twelve years old, on the verge of a storm-wracked adolescence. He will be thrown out of private schools for reasons ranging from arrogance to laziness to venereal disease. Between these schools he will float over the country as if it were a bazaar, picking through a booth here, a booth there, for experiences. He is vain, feckless, and light, with a grandiose sense of himself that buoys and floats him over his own life. It will be years before he knows anything worth knowing. Even at twelve he is a trial for the father but not yet the misery he will become. This son believes he can do whatever he wants to do, and the wounds he receives from his wantoness will soon put him into a trance. For years he will live in that trance, and when he finally wakes as a grown man beginning his own family, he will remember very little of what really happened to him in all those years, and what he does remember will seem to him as remote and mysterious as a fairy story.

So. It is a November afternoon and the father and son are alone in the big house in Alabama. The mother and sister are out of town and it is the cook's and maid's day off. The father is just home from work, still dressed in his suit—striped tie pulled away from his throat—and he is drinking. He is standing in the kitchen drinking bourbon whiskey straight from a bottle that had been hidden in the pantry. The son is there with him.

The son hopes the father will talk to him. What he really hopes is that the suit of armor that is his father will teeter once or twice, creak, and fall over; that it will lie on the kitchen floor, and that birds will finally fly out from its open visor and fill the house. But a conversation will do.

"We're going hunting. Go get your pellet rifle," says the father. He seems happy, and the son feels a thrilling flutter in his stomach.

"Hunting? You mean at Midway? Now?"

Midway, where they go to hunt quail, is a three-hour drive away.

"Not at Midway." The father puts the bottle into a drawer and closes it. "Just come on. Go get your gun."

They take the son's pellet rifle and a shotgun into the backyard. It is a big backyard, with well-spaced oak, hickory, and pine trees. It is a warm evening, almost dusk. The father, still wearing his Brooks Brothers business shirt and tie, carries the side-by-side shotgun into the yard, and the son follows, pumping up his pellet rifle. He watches his father's white shirt move through the darkening air, weaving a little against the black trees, and he tries hard to breathe evenly. He has had the pellet rifle for a year and he has shot a few songbirds and a squirrel or two with it. For two seasons at Midway he has shot a pellet pistol, futilely, at covey rises of quail, and his father has told him that when he kills a quail in that way he will be allowed to shoot a shotgun. Within a year, the son will kill a quail with his pistol and earn the same Winchester shotgun the father is now carrying, and after many more years he will finally learn how to hunt. Now he only wants to know how to kill with purpose, and he can hardly breathe from the suddenness and strangeness of this lesson and from the realization that he wanted it.

The black trees are full of squirrels. Mourning doves, fed and encouraged throughout the neighborhood, clatter in the branches.

"There's a squirrel," says the father, pointing into a hickory tree. "Kill it."

The son can see the squirrel's back humped along a branch. He trembles as he pulls the trigger and misses. The father laughs. The squirrel runs around the tree and they follow it. It is lower now, hugging the trunk, and the son kills it. The father shoots the head off a mourning dove, and when a second one flies out of the trees, he drops it with the second barrel. The Winchester booms insult to the neighborhood, reverberating among the big houses. The father is laughing, laughing. He squeezes the back of the boy's neck with his big hand, and the son can feel in the strength and gaiety of his hand his lifelong unconcern for consequences. They kill another squirrel and two more doves and then, in the dark, they go back inside the house to the big, bright kitchen.

The father takes the bottle from the drawer again and drinks from it. He is all energy and intent now. He pulls out roasting pans, skillets, garlic, bacon. The son has never seen either of his parents cook. In this house meals are cooked behind closed doors, then served in a dining room, by people paid to do those things. He watches the father's banging, spilling, joyful preparation to build a meal for the two of them and is hit by heat coming off of it, as if the father had made a fire in the middle of the room.

They clean the game together at the kitchen table, plucking and drawing the doves, skinning and quartering the squirrels. Pearl gray dove feathers hang in the air. Their hands are bloody. The trash can is full of small entrails. Feathers and fur spill onto the table and floor. Flushed and animated, the father talks and talks about shooting and cooking, fishing and cooking, about using gingerroot with fried bass, duck curry, pompano in a brown bag. He is talking as he wraps the doves in bacon and shoves them into the oven, as he rubs the squirrels with garlic, dips them in egg and cornmeal, and drops them into two cast-iron skillets full of smoking oil, as he pours the last of the whiskey into a water glass, half filling it, to drink with his meal. They eat at the kitchen table off plastic servants' plates. They pull the meat off the bones with their fingers and leave the carcasses on the table, let them fall to the floor. They eat fiercely, as if hungry for more than food—as if they had only one squirrel to share in some deep woods, seated around a bonfire after a long day of danger and adventure. And the son wishes the eating would go on and on. He wishes that his mother and sister would eventually come home and join them around this hearth in the deep woods, and that those woods would be their new home, with just the four of them there, and they could go on and on eating with their hands and talking around the fire his father has built.

The father and son do bend over the meal together for a long time, and when they leave the kitchen they leave it with no dish or pan washed, no spilled blood or dropped bone cleaned up. They just walk away, as if leaving an old campsite.

Later that night the son is upstairs in bed. It is late and the room is dark, but the son is not yet asleep. He realizes that he has been waiting for an answer from his father for a long time and that he has finally been given that answer. His father, he realizes, has told him what he can and cannot have from the father. The son is trying to puzzle out the answer, to get it right, but he can't. And he never does. But years later, after he has many times served himself up to his own children and prayed there was enough to go around, he has an image of his father that night serving what he could of himself on the platter of his manhood to the boy in the kitchen. It is a sturdy, elegant old platter with fine cracks running through it that don't leak, but what is on the platter will leave them both hungry for as long as they live.

Now the father comes into the son's dark bedroom through the bathroom they share and sits on the bed. He is backlit by the open bathroom door and the son cannot see the expression on his face. He sees the big shoulders, the uncombed hair, and he smells whiskey. The father bends and hugs the son to him, holding him lightly, and the son can feel the son in the father as they hold each other. Over the next few years, through the seasickness and fear and hurricane winds of the son's adolescence, the father will do this often, late at night after he has had to whip the son; he will come in late, smelling of whiskey, and hug the son to him, and the hug will feel to the son at those times like iron, like the cold at sea, like the embrace of hopelessness. Now it is just a reassured, grateful goodnight between two family members who for a few hours have shared the joy of being at home together.

Before he died much too young of a stroke, my friend Frank Gafford used to call himself—with great pride and a shining happiness—the *tête de la maison.* "The *tête de la maison,*" he would say in his bad army French, "you're looking at him." That phrase, with its bugle-call sound, stood for everything Frank Gafford was thrilled to be in life, other than a good CPA —husband and father since early in his twenties, guardian, comforter, provider, teacher, skillful organizer of fun. Cooking a Boston butt on the barbecue or driving a car full of kids to the lake, Frank would stroke his ample belly when he told you whom you were looking at, and his eyes would look well nourished and unspeakably delighted with his role of family grower and maintainer, the head of the household.

No one I've ever known was less vain or possession proud than Frank, but he loved to take guests to "walk the property," even in the days when the property occupied by him, his wife, Charlotte, and their three children was just a modest building lot. There would be a flower here to point out, a vine there; at later properties, an herb border over here, over there a brick patio he had built. The details didn't matter. What Frank was forever showing you was the garden where he was blessed to tend to the sweet, swarming blossoms of family life.

Like Frank Gafford, I married and had a family young. I have been a husband and father for as long as I have been an adult. Like Frank I have gloried in those roles and have found nothing else in life half so satisfying or nourishing. For over twenty years my imaginative concept of what it was to be a household head organized both my family's life and mine, and I don't exaggerate or brag when I say I put everything I had into that concept, not out of any formal sense of obligation to it, but because being a father and a husband—a guardian, comforter, provider, teacher, organizer of fun—was my original dream for

myself. From some point very far back in my largely unremem-
bered childhood, a *tête de la maison* who could make a living
writing, at home in a family, was what I wanted to be when I
grew up.

As it happened, I began a little earlier than that. I was a
callow twenty-year-old when a Phi Beta Kappa Miss Alabama
Southern dream girl named Patricia Ellisor walked into the first
meeting of an Oriental literature class I was taking at Birmingham Southern College: Serenely late, she smiled at the professor,
patted her blonde upside-down-tulip hairdo, curled her perfect,
plaid-skirted rear end into a desk, and I knew instantly I was
looking at my future. It took me a while to convince her of that.
She was engaged to someone else and was the star of the campus.
I had just returned to college after a year of traveling around the
country, working at the oddest jobs I could find, and was new
on that campus. I was bulked up then by weight lifting to an
oafish 230 pounds and hard to miss. But day after day in our
class together, this Miss Alabama declined to notice me, until
I stood up one morning at the end of class and somehow took
the whole little wraparound desk with me, ripping it up from
the floor by the bolts. She, like everyone else in the class, was
stopped on her way out of the room by the noise, and she
looked back to where I stood, red-faced, with the desk dangling
from my hips like a draft horse hung up in a plow. She bit her
lower lip and studied me for a moment with her wide blue eyes
as if I were one of the Zen koans we were studying. Then she
smiled, with me rather than at me—a miraculous smile of
amused collaboration over anything that might come up with
either of us from then on.

Within a year Patricia and I were married, and nine

months later we had a son. When this son, whom we named Latham, was only four months old we left Birmingham and moved to Ireland with a few clothes, a crate full of books, and the Winchester double-barreled shotgun my father had given me, the only thing we had of any value other than each other. The idea, a vague one, was to find a thatched-roof cottage somewhere on the west coast where we could live on potatoes and homemade soda bread beside a turf fire while Patricia did a series of paintings as the thesis for her master's degree and I tried to learn how to write, soaked myself in Irish myth and poetry, and read all the books I wanted to read. The roof of the cottage we rented, on the shore of Lough Corrib in Connemara, wasn't thatched, and you can never read all the books you want to read, but otherwise we did pretty much what we set out to do for most of two years, and we began to become a particular kind of family as we did it.

Latham learned how to walk in Ireland, and so did I. Sailors believe that you can know a ship by the first lurch she makes to wind in her sails, her first self-defining forward movement. Latham's first steps were taken in a high-ceilinged yellow room in Dromoland Castle, and they were as surprisingly graceful and determined as he has continued to be.

For myself, I came to Ireland with a fat ass and no interest in exercise other than lifting weights, which I couldn't do there. One day Patricia brought home a wormy little terrier mongrel named Rex, the one-too-many dog of a local farmer who had intended to shoot it that afternoon. At Patricia's urging, I started taking Rex on short walks outside the cottage, trying to housebreak him, liking neither walking nor the dog. But quickly I came to like and then love both, and Rex and I stretched our walks out to five miles each day along the hilly road to Oughterard that ran between stone-walled green fields of sheep and the huge, bright lake full of islands. I found I could think and dream at length on those walks away from paper and books, and patiently mix dreams and thoughts with watching diving ducks on the lake and new lambs in the paddocks and Rex running ahead of me, joyfully, at the heels of some old ewe. Walking was the tempo of our family life then. Walking's leisurely aim to discover, contemplate, and savor was the same as our aim, and learning to do it with Rex gave me a tuning fork to listen to our family grow.

Some years later in Wisconsin, when our tempo had changed and I no longer needed a tuning fork, I gave up walking in favor of running along a dirt road near our house that in the winter was often icy. One January morning Rex, whom we had brought back with us to the States, was run over and killed on that icy road. It was an American farmer finally, rather than an Irish one, who got him, clipping the first flower from the garden Patricia and I had started in Ireland. Bent-legged, hairy-faced, loyal, lionhearted Rex was the first of many dogs to take root and flourish in that garden.

In the book *Iron John*, Robert Bly reminds us of the *hortus conclusus*, or walled garden, of the Middle Ages. These enigmatic, deeply private places with fountains at their centers have provided poets with themes, settings, and metaphors for centuries. Here is Gerard Manley Hopkins describing a nun's longing for the walled garden of taking the veil:

> *I have desired to go*
> *Where springs not fail,*

To fields where flies no sharp or sided hail
And a few lilies blow.
And I have asked to be
Where no storms come,
Where the green swell is in the havens dumb,
And out of the swing of the sea.

A walled garden is refuge, a place of trust and peace, where what you put your hand to bears flower, an ordered shelter "where no storms come," a place of self-reliance and privacy, a heaven for those who believe with Sartre that hell is other people, and a place of perennial growth and blooming where "springs not fail." A good poem or painting is its own walled garden. A cork-lined room was Proust's walled garden, the South Pacific island of Hiva Oa was Gauguin's. Universities can be walled gardens for some people; so can nunneries and monasteries. And families can be walled gardens.

In Ireland Patricia and I had no phone, we knew no one in the country when we first moved there, and we lived a couple of miles from our nearest neighbor—a spritely old rascal with an elf's face named James O'Sullivan who delighted in Latham, called him *"maneen,"* or little man, for Latham's hearty, blond forthrightness, and played with him for hours on his lap, telling him stories about the "little people" who live in the turf bogs and gorse.

Patricia, Latham, and I would huddle together around the house's one space heater on nights when the wind blew off the lake. Patricia made watery little pizzas and I got a local bakery to concoct a kind of hamburger bun to feed part of our hunger for home. I burrowed into reading, writing, and silence and was

sometimes remote, and Patricia was sometimes irritated by that
and by the damp, gray weather. She may even have wondered
sometimes if a small, phoneless cottage in western Ireland was
what she had intended to marry into. And occasionally a blunt,
stubborn streak would surface in her, a slow-to-provoke but
stormy temper, a tendency to sulk, a touchy overprotectiveness
toward her painting that would make me grumpy too with our
complete dependence on each other. But for both of us, the
great majority of our isolated time in Ireland was a sweet spring
planting. Cut off from any kind of life that either of us had
known, and often wrapped in Irish fog, there were only a few
things for us to pay attention to: Painting, writing, reading,
raising a child, and learning how to love each other were the
major ones. Already walled in, we were free to begin the garden
we both wanted around the fountain of our shared dreams for
ourselves and our family. When we moved back to the United
States that garden was in first flower and we carried the walls
with us to protect it.

Our second child, Greta, was born in Iowa City, Iowa,
where I went to graduate school after Patricia had finished her
master's degree work in Athens, Georgia. Next I took a teaching
job in Green Bay, Wisconsin, and Shelby was born there. In
1969, a friend's uncle, who was going into the Vista program
for a year, offered to rent us his house on Lake Sunapee in New
Hampshire. The rent was low, and Patricia and I believed that
after three years in Wisconsin we had enough money saved up
to live on until I could finish a novel, so we moved again.

In Georgia, Iowa, and Wisconsin nothing Patricia or I did
was as important as tending to our growing family garden, and
nothing was as thrilling or as satisfying to either of us as the life

blooming there. Life with our children then was a school of
love, constantly teaching both of us some nuance of affection,
a new sympathy, a new pride. We had some friends during those
years, we went to some parties, we got degrees and earned a
living. We took an occasional trip away from each other and the
kids, and I did some hunting and fishing and closed myself up
alone from time to time to write or read. But none of that was
our life. Our life was propping up Shelby as an infant to let
whichever way he toppled over decide an argument between
Greta and Latham, a practice that earned him the nickname
"Judge" that he still carries. Our life was the sweet warmth of
a child on your lap while watching television, making cinnamon
toast with Greta, taking Latham for his first canoe ride, taking
all three of them out to dinner at Pizza Hut, their popping
energy and curiosity on car trips, the sound of their voices in a
dark house saying goodnight, their slow-breathing bodies asleep,
watching their characters form over difficult decisions, consoling
them, playing cards with them, helping them to dress, reading
to them, seeing new emotions and thoughts cross over their
faces like the shadows of clouds.

　　Nothing had prepared me for the riot of familial love and
happiness Patricia and I harvested in those days, or for the
exhilarating feeling we had of overwhelming completeness, of
needing nothing other than each other and the kids to found the
city of Rome if we wanted, or fly to the moon. No one had ever
told me that men could have access to those particular emotions
and, during that time, every day of my husbanding and fathering
seemed to present me with some new impossible surprise of
feeling.

　　By the time we moved to New Hampshire we were a

completed and self-sufficient family, and nothing on earth was as important to any of us as the others of us. To Patricia and me then the kids were our best friends—as they still are. Latham and Shelby, then as now, were each other's closest confidant. Greta was and is the "glue" of the family.

All three kids were bright, blond, and mouthy, all three had limitless energy, curiosity, and moxie. On long car trips, whenever one of them would get too rambunctious, I'd find a dirt road, let that child out, and invite him or her to run for a few minutes behind the car—which I'd drive at about ten miles an hour—to blow off a little steam. I did this until I realized all three of them loved this particular punishment and were doing everything they could to bring it upon themselves.

All three kids were good natural athletes, and from the time they were toddlers we played all kinds of family sports and games together. We also worked together at chores, took our vacations together, and ate our meals together, even when Patricia and I had adults over. All three were quick to feel, good-humored, generous, and openhearted. And none of them suffered a fool—child or adult—gladly.

Of all the things Patricia and I wanted for them, we wanted most that they be survivors, and they were each urged very young toward independent thought and action, shrugging off pain and getting on with things, and coolness under fire. One of the regular car games we played was called "Survival Situations."

"Okay, Gret," I would say. "You are skiing down a mountain by yourself and you fall. When you try to stand up you realize you can't put any weight on your left foot . . ."

"Where is Latham?"

"He's not there."

"Where are you and Mom?"

"We're not there either. Nobody's there. And it's getting dark. What do you do?"

"Can she make a crutch?" asks Latham.

"She can do anything she wants to do," says Patricia, "but it's her Situation, so let her solve it."

And Greta would.

By the time we moved to New Hampshire, six years after returning from Ireland, I was living—with great pride and a shining happiness—my original dream for myself: I was *tête de la maison* to as close a family unit as I have ever known. The fountain of shared dreams at the center of our walled garden was running full and pure, the garden walls were taller and stronger than ever, the gate locked and the key hidden. But Patricia and I knew already we couldn't keep that gate closed forever. And we knew, but not well enough, that real survival situations awaited all of us just outside it.

3

Patricia and I bought our piece of land on the sea in Nova Scotia in September of 1990. At that time, Latham was twenty-six, living near us in New Hampshire but looking for an opportunity to move west. Greta was twenty-three, living and working with characteristic verve in Jackson Hole, Wyoming, after graduating from Georgetown University. And Shelby was twenty-one and just two college semesters away from being the last one to pack up his room and separate Patricia and me for good from the sweet sustenance of our children living at home.

Within weeks of buying the property we could make out that the dominant feature of our dream for the place was the creation of an environment where, for a few weeks each year, we could reconstitute our family life with our children through daily, self-contained living together. We wanted the place to be not so much a "getaway" as a "get back to"—a site for reclaiming intimacy.

Other features emerged as well. You don't get specific about a dream until you have to, we found, but once you start, it's hard to stop. Less than two years before, Patricia and I had watched out thirty-year relationship blow down around us in a high wind. We had been building a new one carefully from the bottom up, and we saw that we needed a new environment to test its joints for strength. There were other joints in question too: I had recently learned that the ones in both my hips needed replacing. There was a good bit of irony as well as physical pain in that fact. Over the past ten years I had run too much and to too many places. By the time we bought the property in Nova Scotia I was no longer able to run at all, and I no longer wanted to. I wanted to learn to walk again, and the land in Nova Scotia was a good place to do that.

And, finally, the land made us both realize that we wanted to put our tails back in a crack. When we bought the property Patricia and I were a few months on either side of fifty years old, and what we could see from there was looking more and more like the angst-ridden, emptily busy second reel of a foreign film. We and everyone around us seemed to be taking smaller and smaller steps, settling into a life of familiar schedules, herb gardens, and imported vodka. Many of our friends had pulled out of the hike altogether and pitched their tents in the nearest clearing with a pool. Others were still moving but at a cautious shuffle, taking bearings every few feet. No one could blame them for that, God knows. Anyone older than forty knows there are pits out there to fall into, blow-downs to break your legs, deserts to fry you, and rivers to sweep you off your feet and drown you. Anyone over forty knows that the hike now goes through dangerous terrain and has seen friends and family members killed and ruined out there. Taking bearings is trying to outsmart the terrain. Dreaming is dead reckoning, and Patricia and I, never outsmarters, wanted to dream our way ahead now as we had when we were younger. We wanted to go back to a few old dreams for ourselves and our marriage and dead reckon with them into something risky, complicated, big, and all ours to screw up or make work.

By early winter the view from the cape had revealed all of that. That's why we had bought such a big place, we told each other—it had to be big for a dream this size. In fact, shouldn't it be a little bigger? Don't we need a mooring for a boat, a dock for parties, a protected beach for grandchildren someday to use to learn to wade and swim? In that winter of 1991 we went in with some friends and bought seventy more acres, contiguous on the east to what we already had and fronting the pretty little harbor; we worked out the right-of-way to a road into the property and contracted to have it built as soon as the frost was out; and we decided we would build a cabin on the land—build it ourselves as a family so it would be equally ours.

We asked the kids for some of their time in the coming summer and, generously, they gave it to us.

Patricia and I had met Omere Luneau shortly after we moved to New Hampshire, when his wife, Deedee, came to work for us as a baby-sitter. Whenever since then we have undertaken to restore or build anything, from a wood box to a gymnasium, Omere has had a hand in it. When we first came to know him Omere was trying to live himself out of a recent history that included enough unhappy occasions with booze, drugs, and the New Hampshire constabulary to put even the staunchest optimist into a funk. Yet he was never then at a loss for cheerfulness, nor has he ever been since. Omere is relentlessly, fiercely optimistic—whatever is going well is, to him, "cosmic flow," as it should be; whatever is not, is just about to come right. Let's say you're working with him and you split a cedar board with a nail, reducing it to two useless and expensive scraps. "It's okay, it's okay," he will tell you, "we're going to need those pieces for shims in a few minutes." Then when you do need them, the ruined board is back into cosmic flow where it belongs. The universe to Omere is fixable, and he never stops whistling and chattering as he works away on some corner of it. He likes to work with his shirt off, wearing a beret, and during a day's work his untiring, high-energy good nature is wonderfully tonic and contagious. There are better carpenters in New Hampshire and the world than Omere, but none I'd rather see show up in the morning on the job, and it never occurred to us not to involve him in our plans for the property in Nova Scotia.

Omere, Patricia, and I started drawing out sketches in January, and by March we had what we wanted on paper: a cabin twenty feet by twenty-four feet with a saltbox tin roof over a living/eating room with a sleeping loft above, a small bathroom, and an open workshop shed in the back. Our original rough plan for the cabin looked like this:

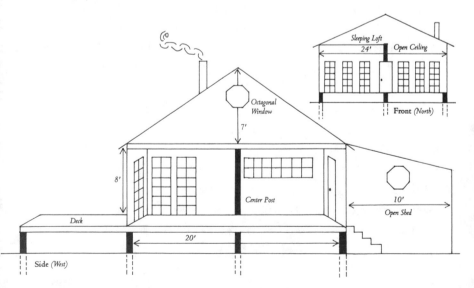

Because we wanted to avoid putting in a full septic system, we planned on laying a small leach field to take care of the "gray" water from the shower and kitchen and bathroom sinks. For a toilet we decided to go with an Omere-conceived "indoor outhouse." We would sink a pressure-treated, bottomless plywood box, four feet wide and eight feet deep, into the ground beneath a mounted toilet seat, and fill two feet of this box with three-quarter-inch pea-stone gravel. A vent pipe would carry off odor; liquid wastes would drain through the gravel into the soil; and solids would sit on the gravel and dry out. It looked great on paper.

We would get our power from a generator. With the help of an electrician friend Omere and I came up with a wiring plan. We figured out wattage requirements and looked at various generators, finally deciding on a 3,500-watt Honda with an electric starter. "This baby's a Cadillac," said the salesman, starting it up in the showroom. "See how quiet it is?" he shouted at me.

Noise aside, a generator is a miraculous thing. Knowing virtually nothing about the alchemy of electricity, I was as delighted as a headhunter to learn you could carry this thing onto an iceberg, say, put some gas in it, turn it on, and run a vacuum cleaner or a toaster. I fooled with the Honda all winter. If it was going to let us take a shower and Cuisinart a salad dressing in a blueberry field a mile from the nearest electrical outlet, I wanted to get to know it.

I also made lists of what we would need and want to take with us to Nova Scotia. My aim in these lists was to be ample rather than austere. Life on the cape for this first summer, I reckoned, would be Spartan enough, particularly before we got the cabin built, and I saw no need to avoid including a few

emollients in the planning. In this tendency, of course, I was
flying us in the face of that great but stingy cabin builder,
Thoreau.

The house Thoreau built for himself on Walden Pond in
1845 was "ten feet wide by fifteen long, and eight-feet posts,
with a garret and a closet, a large window on each side, two trap
doors, one door at the end, and a brick fireplace opposite." This
place cost him twenty-eight dollars twelve-and-a-half cents to
build. For what he needed and wanted to live there he paid
nothing, and it was a slim list of goods: "a bed, a table, a desk,
three chairs, a looking glass three inches in diameter, a pair of
tongs and andirons, a kettle, a skillet, and a frying pan, a dipper,
a washbowl, two knives and forks, three plates, one cup, one
spoon, a jug for oil, a jug for molasses, and a japanned lamp."
Thoreau went to Walden to live as simply as possible—meeting
only his needs for food, shelter, clothing, and fuel, and those
only in the most basic ways—in order to free himself up for an
unbothered life of the mind. He believed that: "Most of the
luxuries, and many of the so-called comforts of life, are not only
not indispensable, but positive hindrances to the elevation of
mankind. With respect to luxuries and comforts, the wisest have
ever lived a more simple and meager life than the poor."

Patricia and I too wanted to reorganize our lives around
a new place in order to live more simply (though neither of us
was much interested in meager), but together with our kids, we
found, we had a good many more needs to meet than did
Thoreau. I spent much of the winter going through the gear I
already owned and poring over camping catalogs, trying to
identify and assemble, within the limits of our budget, every

item I could think of to keep us well housed and well fed, warm, productive, and entertained while the cabin was being built.

I ordered two four-person Pine Tree Lodge tents from L.L. Bean and borrowed a third expedition tent from a friend. Thoreau's narrow handmade bed became for us Swedish folding cots with mattresses and down sleeping bags. We would bathe with a big plastic bag that hangs from a tree and showers you in sun-warmed water, rather than in Walden Pond. In addition to kettle, skillet, and frying pan, we would take along a propane grill and charcoal smoker, and Thoreau's few cooking and eating implements multiplied on my list into lobster-claw crackers, corkscrews, and a garlic press. Thoreau had a few simple tools; we had more and much improved ones, organized by Omere, including a chain saw, a brush cutter, and a pneumatic nail gun. Thoreau's sole source of entertainment at Walden Pond outside his thoughts and his writing were several books he took with him, chiefly Homer's *Iliad.* We would take that book and others, too, for our entertainment, but also a twenty-one-foot Starcraft Islander boat, a sea kayak, a windsurfer, a small sailboat, an inflatable raft, mountain bikes, water skies, fishing tackle, a giant kite, wet suits and snorkeling gear, board games, and a football.

Rather than feeling ashamed of all that dispensable recreational equipment, I liked imagining Thoreau having some of it at Walden Pond and secretly enjoying it—taking a spin around the little lake on a windsurfer after a morning of writing, maybe—indulging a secret playfulness that no one in Concord could suspect in the stern and parsimonious author of these words: "As for the Pyramids, there is nothing to wonder at in

them so much as the fact that so many men could be found
degraded enough to spend their lives constructing a tomb for
some ambitious booby, whom it would have been wiser and
manlier to have drowned in the Nile, and then given his body
to the dogs."

By late April I had pretty much finished filling up the
garage with gear, and our plans were set. Latham, Greta, and
Shelby, Greta's boyfriend, Rob McLeod, Shelby's college room-
mate Nick, and Patricia and I would drive up to Nova Scotia
in early June. We would get a camp established on the land, and
Omere would join us there a couple of days later. Omere had
volunteered himself and his tools for three weeks to help us
build the cabin. He and Rob, a semiprofessional carpenter in
Wyoming, would provide the know-how; the rest of us, willing
hands and backs. Nick would be with us for two weeks. Greta
would have to leave in mid-July, and Shelby a couple of weeks
later. The rest of us planned to stay until the end of August.

In early May, Patricia, Omere, and I flew up to Nova
Scotia to order the materials for the cabin, pick a building site
for a 'dozer to clear and level, and meet Tom Mattie, who was
going to do the bulldozing and road building before we came
back up in June. Tom was a solid, instantly likable man in his
early fifties with a kind face and a gently ingratiating manner.
The day we met him at the property, Saint Georges Bay was still
completely locked up in a vast, white jumble of ice and a strong
wind blew off of it, carrying a little cold rain. As he walked with
us over the mile of brush that would become a long shale
driveway linking our cabin to the public road, Tom talked about
road building as if it were an art form, using a lot of idiosyncratic body English and with such obvious relish for this project

that Patricia, Omere, and I knew immediately that we'd get a good road.

Up at the blueberry shack the wind was blowing so hard we had to lean against it, and the gray-white bay of ice stretching below us was wild and thrilling with personality. We showed Tom where we wanted the cabin site cleared and leveled, just north of the blueberry shack near the spruce line at the rear of the property, leaving the entire cape in front of us. And we asked him about a well. He would dig it with a backhoe, he said, as near the cabin site as possible. And how would he know where to dig? He had a friend who was not too bad as a dowser, he told us; Tom would get him up here to find a good vein of water with his willow wand. Whenever Tom Mattie talked into the wind he kept his hands cupped over his mouth. After a while he explained that his new teeth were late coming in from Halifax, and the wind was a little cold on his gums. We could walk back down to the car, we suggested. No, no hurry, said Tom. He and two of his brothers had been in the excavating business in this area for thirty years, and he knew Edna and Walter Boudreau well, but he had never been up here on the cape before. Now that he was here and had seen it, he said, he was in no hurry at all to leave.

We also needed to get one final right-of-way for the road from a man named Ralph DeCoste, who lived just up the road from the Boudreaus, near the fishing wharf. It was a Saturday morning when Patricia, Omere, and I stopped in to see him, and when he opened his back door children seemed to boil out around him. There were five of them—ages four through twelve, we learned—all curious, polite, friendly kids. Ralph and his pretty wife, Maria, who held a baby on her hip, talked to us outside in their yard. Their kids swirled around us on bikes and tricycles, showing us new kittens and talking, all of them, a mile a minute.

It was the day after we met with Tom Mattie. Overnight the ice had gone out on the bay and, from the DeCoste yard, we could watch great chunks of it float northward on an outgoing tide. The weather had turned warm and sunny and Ralph DeCoste had his shirt off. He and Maria were in their midthirties. Ralph worked as a computer consultant in Antigonish and Maria was a nurse at the hospital there. They were bright, funny, engaging people, and Patricia and I liked them and their kids immediately.

Were we really putting in a road all the way up to the blueberry shack, they wanted to know? And was it for a trailer park development, as they had heard rumored? We assured them it was not and told them our plans. In that case, they said, they had no problem with giving us right-of-way over a piece of their land that the road would cross. That piece of land, they said, had a shack on it on a bluff overlooking the bay and we were welcome to stay in the shack for as long as we wanted when we came back up in June.

We left New Hampshire on June 7 in a convoy of two trucks and a Suburban. Patricia and I led off, towing the twenty-one-foot motorboat. Greta and her boyfriend, Rob, drove the old Ford pickup I had bought for fifteen hundred dollars, and Latham, Shelby, Shelby's friend Nick, and Nick's dog, Crash, brought up the rear in Shelby's pickup. Riding with me, as they did everywhere I went, were my two bird dogs: a five-year-old golden retriever named Fields and a Llewelyn setter called Arthur. As we pulled out it occurred to me and Patricia that although we were driving away from a restored Colonial house full of books, antiques, and old rugs, a pantry and freezer full of specialty food items, a cellar full of good wines, a pond full of trout and pastures full of sheep, her art studio, my gym, two offices, a world-class caretaker, and a fax machine, we had with us everything and everyone we needed to start over from scratch.

We also had with us an excellent crew for this particular project. In Omere and Rob we had real building talent and experience. Latham and Shelby had some experience with construction and all the others of us could at least swing a hammer. In Patricia, Greta, and myself we had three better than average cooks. Nick, Greta, Latham, and Shelby could all play the guitar and sing. Everyone in the group had spent lots of time in the outdoors and had done some camping: Everyone could build a fire, use an outhouse comfortably, pitch a tent, go to sleep with coyotes howling, and deal with weather. And no one with us was married to television, nightlife, or the telephone. Starting out, I knew that we had Omere's and Rob's boundless good spirits with us, Latham's sense of humor, Shelby's and Patricia's sweetness, and Greta's grit—everything we needed, in fact, in human resources as well as gear to resettle Nova Scotia if necessary. But that didn't stop me—occasionally during the winter and more frequently as we got closer to departure—from entertaining a host of nameless fears in the middle of the night. At three or four in the morning it would seem I was crazily putting much too much at risk: Broken limbs would loom out of the bedroom dark, chain-saw accidents, weeks of rain, irreparable quarrels, and—the worst of these nightmares—the utter defeat of having the summer separate rather than unite us.

Our first day on the road suggested some of my fears

might not be unfounded. In Bangor, Maine, I sideswiped a parked car with the boat trailer. Farther north, in Calais, I came within inches of plowing into the back of another car that had stopped suddenly to make a turn, and a few miles further down the road, Canadian Customs and Immigrations took an astonished look at the goods we were carrying, supposed we might be bringing all these grills, coolers, plastic chairs, tents, sleeping bags, boats, and tools into Canada to sell, and almost turned us back. After three hours of explanations, twelve hours after leaving New Hampshire, we crossed into New Brunswick and stopped at the first motel we could find. That night I slept through all my nightmares.

The next day's drive went more smoothly, and we were in Antigonish by four thirty. We bought some basic grocery supplies and three buckets of Kentucky Fried Chicken and drove on for the property. It was showering and gray in Antigonish. Superstitiously, I wanted our children to see the property for the first time with sun on it and the sea. As we started east, a band of clearing sky appeared ahead of us, but it seemed a long way off. Twenty minutes later we turned off the Trans-Canada, drove through the small village of Monastery, crossed the railroad tracks and the Tracadie River, and turned left onto the road to Barrio Beach. This patched, sand-colored old road ran through East Tracadie, the little community of some thirty houses that we were moving into. It passed Tom Mattie's house and wound by small, neat bungalows, hay fields, and a few farms. Just before Ralph DeCoste's house the road makes a crest that sideswipes you every time with a view of Tracadie Harbor, the fishing wharf, and the bay beyond that is so perfectly composed, abundant, and serene that you seem to see it from a

trance. Directly above this crest was the seam between clouds
and clearing sky, and as we topped the hill the sun slid out and
lit the harbor, the wharf, the island of spruces on the far side
of the harbor, and the bay.

I hit the brakes on the Suburban. Patricia took my hand
and squeezed it. After a moment I drove on slowly, and we
could feel the kids behind us, cresting the hill to this magical
view, then passing through it as if it were a suddenly illuminated
doorway, following us into the dead-reckoned dream on the
other side.

We stopped to drop off the boat in Ralph and Maria
DeCoste's backyard and to introduce our family to theirs. The
DeCoste kids swarmed over the boat and around our convoy,
making instant friends with Greta. Ralph and Maria wished us
a good night's sleep in their shack on the bluff and urged us to
use their bathroom and phone whenever we needed.

It was just after seven when we turned for the first time
onto our fine new shale road and drove up it slowly to the
blueberry shack. The sky was now a washed blue, the sun
lowering over Cape George, and the sea steely and flat. I let
Arthur and Fields out of their kennels. The kids got out of the
trucks, and everyone, dogs and people, just stood there for a
long moment looking around without making a sound.

"Well, what do you think?" said Patricia finally. It was a
big moment for her—and for me.

"Jesus, it's really out here," said Latham after a pause. His
voice was small. He seemed to be speaking for all of them, even
Fields and Arthur, who sat on their tails looking worried. And
though the response didn't make me happy, I knew what he was
getting at: However beautiful, with a cold dusk coming on, the

light flattening, and the still raw road disappearing downhill through a mile of coyote habitat, the place did have an unsettling feel of remoteness to it.

Feeling suddenly exhausted, totally winded in the heart and head, I walked over to a big, ugly pit that had been backhoed near the building site. I looked down into the well Tom Mattie had dug for us: It was as dry as a bone.

Greta came over then and took my arm. "It's beautiful, Dad," she said. "I think it's the most beautiful place I've ever seen."

The DeCoste shack sat forty feet from the edge of a sheer bluff overlooking the bay. It had no running water, electricity, or heat, and with only two small rooms and a sleeping loft, it was snug for seven people and three dogs, but it was a welcome shelter for the night—and you couldn't beat the view. We pulled on pile jackets and ate fried chicken and drank beer on the bluff as the sun went down. Then Greta, Latham, and Nick broke out their guitars. We lit a couple of propane lamps and had a good sing in the little shack, and I decided to quit worrying about the consensus of silent nervousness on the cape.

The next morning at first light I drove up to the top of the hill to check on the gear we had left there and found such a perfect, bell-clear dawn that I stayed for two hours unpacking boxes, clearing brush for the tent platforms, and watching sea gulls dip and soar over the end of the cape. After breakfast at the DeCoste shack we all went back up to the land together. It was a brilliant morning, the breeze fresh, the sea wrapping the cape in deep, vivid blue; and this morning there seemed to be proprietary grins on more faces than just mine as we began the exhilarating work of starting from scratch to house ourselves on our land.

*   *   *

The first order of business was to organize a tent camp to live in while the cabin was being built. We began by clearing a half acre of brush around the blueberry shack and building three 12′ × 12′ platforms out of pressure-treated 2′ × 6′ boards for the tents to sit on. Patricia and I left this work during the afternoon to fill every container we had with water from the DeCostes' hose. Maria had baked us two apple pies. We went by to see Mary Mattie, Tom's wife, and she had a fresh loaf of bread for us. We stopped in to say hello to Edna and Walter Boudreau, and Edna had made us a potful of her storied seafood chowder. And Michael Delory and his wife Anne, who lived across the street from Edna and Walter, waved us over and gave us sixteen boiled lobsters.

All of this neighborly largesse put me into such a blessing-counting frame of mind that I only smiled and nodded later that afternoon when Tom Mattie drove up to tell us what we already knew—the well dowser had missed. Tom had gone as deep as he could go with the backhoe, and we now had an eight-hundred-dollar dry hole in the ground. We could have the dowser try again, and Tom would dig another hole, or we could drill for the water, at close to twenty dollars a foot. Rob and Latham and I talked it over: A drilled well not only would be expensive but would require an expensive submersible pump. The worst case that way was a deep and very pricey well, but we would definitely have water. The worst case the other way was a collection of eight-hundred-dollar dry holes. There were a couple of marshes and a little brook on the cape, Rob pointed out, indicating shallow groundwater; he believed the driller would hit water within fifty feet. One hundred feet, said Latham. I said a hundred and fifty, and we put up a fifteen-dollar pool on it.

Let's drill it, I told Tom Mattie.

"I'll have him here tomorrow," he said. "Good decision."

We spent another night at the DeCoste shack and dined on Michael Delory's lobsters, fresh bread, and apple pie. The next day Patricia and I went into town to shop. It was a hot, breezy, beautiful afternoon on the cape when we got back. The platforms were finished, the big, dark-green tents pitched on them, and the well was drilled. Latham met me at the car. "The good news is they found all the water we need at ninety-seven feet. The bad news is you owe me five bucks from the pool, and our generator isn't big enough to work the submersible pump. We need five thousand watts. Here's a beer."

I worked on putting together a site for bonfires for the rest of the afternoon. I dug a big fire pit, ringed it with shale rocks from the beach, made seats around the pit out of driftwood logs, and enjoyed the imaginative pleasure of creating this hearth of future warmth, brightness, music, and collective dreaming. Just as I finished the pit Omere drove up. I was delighted to see him get out of his truck, brandishing his optimism as always with a big grin and a jaunty walk.

"Great campfire area," he said.

"I thought you'd like it."

"So, *que pasa?*"

"Camp's all set. We'll stay up here tonight and you can sleep in the DeCostes' shack. We had to drill the well . . ."

"Good. Probably better water."

"And go with a submersible pump . . ."

"Great—more dependable."

"But the generator won't run it. We need fifteen hundred more watts."

"My friend J.T. is coming up in a week. We'll get him to bring a five thousand and I can get the Honda guy to take ours back on trade. I've been thinking we needed a little more juice for all the power tools, so that's perfect."

"Weather's been great."

"You see? There you go," said Omere. "Cosmic flow."

Over the next few days the weather stayed good and we got a lot of work done. We built a plywood deck around two sides of the blueberry shack and extended a lean-to roof off of it that we covered with a tarp. After rigging the three open sides with tarps that could be rolled down and hooked to the deck, we had a roofed and decked cooking/eating area eight feet wide by twenty feet long that could be left open in nice weather and walled with the rolled tarps against rain or wind. The back wall of this area was the east side of the blueberry shack, along which we built a counter for serving and eating and shelves for holding dishes and pots and pans. We made the inside of the shack into a pantry, installed a propane refrigerator in it, and cut a window in the east wall for passing things out to the deck. With the refrigerator and two big coolers, the grill, a smoker, and a two-burner gas stove we had a big volume and efficient kitchen. We ate at the counter and a wooden picnic table, washed dishes in DeCoste hose water heated in a big lobster pot, and illuminated the lean-to kitchen at night with two Coleman lamps.

Ralph DeCoste gave us an old outhouse that had been standing unused behind his shack. We brought it up in a truck, cut a new moon in its door, and installed it over a three-foot pit in the spruce woods at the end of a little path that twisted through wild rosebushes and Indian pear trees.

We built freestanding clothes shelves for the tents, a communal washstand, a tarp-and-board housing for the generator. There was also grocery shopping and laundry to do, ordering and picking up building materials, preparing meals and washing dishes, and all of us shared more or less equally in those chores as we did in the manual work. In the evenings we would bathe under the Sunshower or in the beaver pond down by the DeCostes' shack, drink a little beer or rum, build a bonfire and cook a big, collaborative meal, then sit around the fire to sing and tell stories for an hour or two before carrying a flashlight back to the tents and the sleeping bags.

By the end of our first week on the land we had established a good working schedule and put together a comfortable tent camp. We had laid out the cabin's foundation area with batter boards and string lines, had most of our building materials delivered to the site, and sunk railroad ties as piers for the cabin to rest on. We had had day after day of perfect weather—clear hot days and cool, starry nights—and very few hitches. By the end of that week we were organized, ready to begin building the cabin, and feeling pretty much in control of everything. In fact, this building your own house on wild land was looking pretty much like a snap when, a week to the day after we had arrived in Nova Scotia, the biggest storm of the summer came crashing in out of the northwest, throwing lobster boats up onto docks on Prince Edward Island and nearly snuffing out our camp.

The rain and wind started at night and lasted for close to

forty-eight hours: over six inches of rain; steady fifty-mile-an-hour winds with gusts to eighty. There was nowhere to go but the tents, and being in them was almost as wet and much noisier than being in a small boat on a rough sea. The tents held up, if barely. We lost two of the tarps on the lean-to, and meals were such a laughably uncomfortable effort that for two days we got along mostly on peanut butter sandwiches. Shelby, Latham, and Nick were sharing the tent I had borrowed from a friend. It was older and leakier than the two new L.L. Bean tents, and the boys simply stayed in it, in their soggy cots, covered with everything they could find, until the storm ended.

Storms happen outside houses, and houses just sit still in storms, pretending not to notice what's going on. But a tent fights for its life in a good storm, clapping and popping, moaning and straining, and that fight brings the storm right inside. In a tent in a big storm you are always wiping up water, picking up something that's been knocked over, running outside to tighten one guy rope or loosen another, and figuring a course of action for when the thing finally blows away with you inside it. None of this makes for sound sleep, and a day or two of it can put an edge on your mood and even make you start considering alternative shelter. We had a number of visitors on the first day of our big blow who offered us their houses, and the word "motel" might even have come up, but Patricia and I wanted to last it out and everyone else decided to stay with us.

Once that decision was made a kind of determined gaiety set in. That night Patricia, Omere, Rob, Greta, and I grilled up a windy supper of burgers and beans, drank some Nova Scotia moonshine, cranked up a little Bonnie Raitt to keep warm by, and danced in the rain on the lean-to deck. And after Omere drove back down to the DeCoste shack and Greta and Rob went off to bed, Patricia and I put on a tape of golden hits by The Platters and slow danced with gloves on as the tents thumped and the wind howled along to "The Great Pretender" and "The Magic Touch."

On the afternoon of the second day Omere and I walked out to the end of the cape along the cliffs down to the eastern harbor and back to the camp through the woods to the south. Standing on the cape, leaning into the wind and the rain, was as exhilarating and loud as a good rock concert—the bay whipped into parallel lines of whitecapped breakers, the wind screeching through holes in the cliff. The woods coming back were foggy green, dripping, and they smelled of balsam; buoyant and wet, Omere and I bushwhacked through them back to the camp.

"It's good to get the worst over early," Omere said happily, as we stepped into the clearing and looked over the drowned and whipping tents and the tarpless lean-to.

Rob stuck his head out of his tent to tell me that Patricia and Greta had walked down to the DeCoste house to get some exercise and take a bath. They wanted me to pick them up at five.

Patricia has a way of going unaffectedly cheerful in emergencies. When I cut an artery on a piece of window glass in Ireland, she told me happy little stories about a fair she had been to in Oughterard that day while she kept a dishrag tourniquet tight around my arm on the long drive to a hospital in Galway. Being tested wafts her up somehow and makes her eyes shine. She had been cheering and tireless over the past forty hours, helping reinforce the tents, making coffee, carrying hot soup and

sandwiches to the boys, and I knew she hadn't slept for more
than a couple of hours during that time. When I walked into
the DeCoste house she was curled up snoozing on a bench in
their entrance hall, her hair still wet from her first bath in a week.
That hair needed some attention; she had not put on makeup
since we arrived in Nova Scotia; and the layers of old work
clothes she had on gave her a bit of a bag lady look there on the
bench. But Patricia has never once in her life needed hairdos or
makeup or stylish clothes to be beautiful, and she didn't need
them then.

I looked down at her long-loved, sleeping face and thought
of all the worry that could be there now but wasn't. I thought:
You and I have lived in a lot of places and we have learned—
God, have we learned—how to weather storms.

4

At any given time we are the sum of all our new beginnings, including every house we have ever moved to or built. For better or worse, dream husks pile up around us after a while in any house, and a move from one to another can be an act almost as optimistic as having a child—a blind jump to a place where life just might be better, richer, and more precious than it is where we already are; where, at least, the dreams are fresh.

The less brought along on such a move the better. Drug addicts call it "pulling a geographic" when someone just hauls the same old baggage across country to deal with in a new place. A move into change starts with arson.

The place we brought Latham to after he was born was an underground apartment just off the campus of Birmingham Southern College, where I was finishing my undergraduate degree. This cave had black walls and a year-round moldy odor, but it was cool in the worst Alabama heat and it was cheap. Patricia and I had moved into it from a garage apartment behind my parents' big house on the other side of town. We were moving away, we hoped forever, from debutante parties and country clubs and to the beginning of a family, an academic, artistic life, and friends who were not lawyers and businessmen.

The cave housed those modest dreams well. Latham's blond head and blue eyes glowed against the black kitchen wall as Patricia rocked his baby seat with one hand and fried chicken with the other. In the living room, Tommy Tucker, Jimmy Nash, and I played hours of a kind of floor hockey game we invented called "Sco'!" using one of our wallets for a puck. The living room was long and narrow, with a slick floor, and none of the wallets ever had enough money in it to slow it down. Day and night Martin Hames, Eddie Entrekin, Jim Allen, and others would come and go through the cave, talking of Ionesco, Samuel Beckett, Robert Lowell, and Franz Kline. The night Latham was born his four godfathers all waited with me at the hospital through every minute of Patricia's twenty-two-hour labor and delivery, then we went back to the cave and celebrated with a six-pack of cheap beer and a game of "Sco'!"

Greta was brought home from the hospital to an old, wide-porched farmhouse in the cornfields of Iowa, where Patricia and I dreamed of being—finally, both of us—out of graduate school, of working at painting and writing, and of my finding some job good enough to let us buy a secondhand station wagon and some new luggage.

I still had my father's Winchester with me in Iowa, and I used it there like a hungry man stuffing food into his face with both hands. For three years before I had been on a self-imposed diet of W. B. Yeats's verse plays and Walter Savage Landor's poetry, of trying to write wispy, melancholy poems and plays myself, talking an off-the-rack brand of expatriate, academic radicalism, and analyzing European novels down to their comma patterns. One night in Ireland I actually talked to Thomas Mann in my sleep. There was not much animal protein in that diet, and my response to what seemed to be more of the same fare in graduate school was to run for the nearest pork-tenderloin sandwich. With Dick Wentz usually, I hunted almost every day of the two seasons I was in Iowa for quail, pheasant, ducks and geese, even illegal doves. Plenty of days I would hunt twelve hours straight. When there was nothing better to shoot, I'd go looking for carp with a bow and arrow, and too often I'd get to my classes in Iowa City late, dressed in bloody field clothes, and sit in the back in a happy, overfed stupor, dreaming about jump-shooting wood ducks on the Iowa River.

Hunting and fishing first became for me then the stuff of secret, long-distance dreaming, too. Sitting on the farmhouse porch with Patricia on a cooling summer evening, while Latham pushed a wooden truck across the floor and Greta tried to learn to flop over in her playpen, I'd drink a beer, look out over the corn and soybean fields, and illicitly imagine a grander house somewhere from which I might sally now and then to the moors of Scotland to gun for driven grouse, or to the Great Barrier Reef to mix it up with thousand-pound marlin. Then I'd pick up Greta, look into her busy, snub-nose face, know instantly and exactly where the center of my life was, and think there couldn't be much harm in such unlikely dreaming.

In Green Bay, Wisconsin, I got the good job Patricia and I had dreamed of back in Iowa. We also got the station wagon and the new luggage, and the home Shelby was brought to after his birth was a nice suburban rental on the Fox River. We had mostly struggling professional artists for friends in Green Bay, and our major dream for ourselves in that Fox River house was to find a way to support ourselves and our now completed family through painting and writing.

My job was directing a Title III government program that brought visual artists, musicians, dramatists, dancers, and writers from all around the country to teach their arts in the Brown County, Wisconsin, school system. The program had a three-year lifespan, and the big question facing Patricia and me during that time—as it did the fifteen or so other artists working with us—was what to do when the program ended. We would sit up late after barbecues on the back deck of the Fox River house, with Latham and Greta asleep in our laps and Shelby sleeping between us in his crib, talking with Heine and Karon Hagemeister, Bob and Mona Ray, Bud and Karen Beyer, Bob Phillips and Olie Olson about the lives of committed creativity we would all live and reassuring ourselves that none of us would ever sell out—not for money, not for fame, not even for the Australian marlin fishing of my secret dreaming.

When the Title III program ended, Patricia and I had the choice of moving to Washington, D.C., and taking a cushy job with the Ford Foundation, or to New Hampshire and gambling all our savings on my writing a first novel. We never even thought about it: We dead reckoned to New England.

Patricia, Latham, Greta, and Shelby are down on the dock swimming in the brackish river that winds through a salt marsh to the sea. I am in the big house, nude in the midday South

Carolina low-country heat and talking on the phone to my agent. He is telling me that my second book, a nonfiction book about bodybuilding, has just made the *New York Times* bestseller list. This is astonishing, gratifying news, and my agent and I are gloating over it. As it happens, I am in a good place to gloat: a two-thousand-acre, seaside plantation estate that has been lent to us for a month by a friend. And, too, gloating is becoming something of a habit. The movie version of my first novel is due out in a few months, and I am writing the narration for the movie version of this second book, now a bestseller.

We have lived in New Hampshire for six years now, and for the last four of those years we have had so much good luck that Patricia and I haven't yet noticed that our garden gate is now standing wide open.

My agent is telling me I should fly to New York for a party a particularly lovely actress is giving when I hear Greta scream and Patricia shriek my name.

"I have to go . . ."

"She really wants to meet you. Can you come?"

I'm actually thinking about how I can swing this trip to New York when I drop the phone and run for the door. Running is something I do all the time now, and I am through the glass doors and across the thirty yards of grass between the house and the dock before Patricia has shouted my name three times. She is standing on the dock holding Shelby; Latham and Greta are in the water yelling. I dive off the dock in a full sprint, come up between the two kids and tow them in to shallow water.

"What the hell happened?" I ask Greta after I get my breath.

"Latham started screaming. I thought it was a shark. . . . Why are you naked?"

We check Latham over and find a couple of red welts on his lower back where a Portuguese man-of-war has grazed him. He and Greta are calm now and want to go back into the water. The emergency is over and I was only a little late for it. I wrap a towel around my waist and sit down on the dock.

"Do you want to go to New York next week?" I ask my wife. "I need to go up for a day or two."

"No," she says. "But you go ahead."

The New Hampshire house we returned to from South Carolina was a fine, big, red one in the middle of an apple orchard. We rented it, but at this point we could have bought it had it been for sale. We now had a baby-sitter/housekeeper working for us, a color television, and a few good paintings other than Patricia's. I had more than one fly rod and shotgun now, and even the Old Town canoe I had wanted for years and a Jeep Wagoneer to carry it. And I had begun to travel a little to fish and shoot, often with my father.

Patricia and I were traveling more often, too, and now we usually left the kids at home. We went to Greece, to Italy, on an eating tour of France, and every month or so we went to New York or Los Angeles where, after a while, we were on pretty fast tracks without having any idea why. For some reason I was having suits made for me by a fancy little tailor in New York and Patricia was shopping at Hermès. For some reason our supper bills were suddenly in three figures, and we would find ourselves sitting around big, crowded tables at Elaine's or Dan Tana's ordering fried squid at midnight in a hubbub of movie and literary talk, starlets practicing English accents, and people bubbling out of the bathrooms with wired eyes and little white powder mustaches.

A best-selling exercise book and a loan from my father finally let us buy our own home in 1979. It was everything we had dreamed of it being: a big, beautifully restored Colonial house, a separate barn to turn into a studio, writing office, and gym, thirty acres with pastures for sheep and a horse, a pond for trout, a tennis court. Our dreams for our first-owned house had always been centered around the things we could do there with the kids. This was a wonderful place for children, and Patricia and I did do there everything we had dreamed of doing with them. But by then there were a lot of other people in our lives, and we invited many of those people into this fine, new home and into the family garden we kept there, and after a while there were people standing around everywhere in the house and the garden, whole house parties of them from New York and Los Angeles, eating canapés, drinking wine, and chatting.

There were models and big-game hunters, actors and charter-boat captains, photographers and athletes, writers and adventurers, cinematographers, Wall Street brokers, sculptors, professors, and producers. Many of these people were attractive, lighthearted, talented, and amusing, and we and the kids had great fun barbecuing with them and putting on tennis tournaments and "game days" with tug-of-war and egg tosses on the lawn and swimming races in the pond. We would take them out on Lake Sunapee in our old wooden motorboat, or climb a mountain with them, or introduce them to bass fishing on a local pond. We made them Bellinis and Colonels and cooked frittatas for them on Sunday mornings and brought them the *New York Times* on the porch with their coffee. We had many good times with all these people in our new house, but too often we had a hard time finding each other in the crowd. Too often the parties and weekends would go on too long, and Patricia and I would get bitchy with each other over that, or over some walk in the woods I might have taken with a model, some odd inflection to a good-bye kiss she might have given a sculptor on his way back to New York.

Latham went off to boarding school the year after we bought this house, beginning the annual school-year loss for Patricia and me that within five years would claim all three kids. The local school system being what it was, going away to preparatory schools was the best thing for our children, and they knew that and wanted to go. But leaving home was painful for all three of them, and it was a constant dull ache of loss for Patricia and me.

During the years that our children lived at home all five of us felt safe, whole, and capable of anything. Whatever house we were in, the family was our true, safe harbor, and in it none of us could conceive of a storm that might wreck us or a journey we couldn't make. When first Latham, then Greta and Shelby, went away to boarding school, it left all of us feeling suddenly cast-off and adrift, contingent and imperiled—reliant on the dangerous world instead of each other. On vacations and during the summer we would get the safety and wholeness back, and sometimes even our old sense that anything we did, as long as we did it together, was charmed. But then the vacation or summer would end and the kids would return to prep school or college, leaving me and Patricia feeling vulnerable and anxious, on opposite sides of a black hole of loss that widened every year, so that before long it was hard for us to take each other's hand across it.

Patricia tried to ignore this widening hole by putting more and more of herself and her time into her painting and sculpture. I tried to run across it, chasing a changed dream of myself. This dream had the force and shininess of being truly new, and yet I could remember it forming out of my childhood, from dusk on an Alabama bass lake, and from snappy January mornings walking up to a quail dog stuck and quivering on point like an arrow in a tree trunk, and from an evening of shooting backyard doves and squirrels with my father and then huddling over them for a meal and a talk. With my kids away from home I lost myself as a *tête de la maison.* And when my second novel didn't do as well critically or commercially as I believed it should have, I pouted and lost myself as a writer. At age forty I started over on a new dream for myself, and what I wanted from it was sport, travel, and action. This house, I decided— this end-of-the-road family dream house—was the one I would finally begin to sally from.

While Patricia retreated deeper and deeper into her studio and her subconscious, I threw as many balls as I could find into the air and then ran around keeping them there. I worked freelance for ABC's "The American Sportsman" because it took me, finally, marlin fishing in Australia. I took up rock and ice climbing and scuba diving. I angled magazine stories about helicopter skiing through herds of caribou on the Gaspé Peninsula and documenting wild grizzly bears in Montana, about living for a week with a woman-led street gang in the Bronx and diving with tiger sharks on the Great Barrier Reef. I fished in Mexico, Canada, Alaska, and Central and South America, and shot birds in almost as many places. I hunted wild turkeys in south Alabama with a drug-crazed country music star and swam with mating tarpon in Homossassa Bay, tried out hang gliding and built up enough frequent flyer miles to fly free to Mars.

During this period I wasn't always careful or smart. I offered to fight a number of men in blue with guns on their hips, drank too much whiskey, smoked Honduran cigars, and used an illegal drug or two. I developed a hair-trigger contempt for psychiatrists and the growing number of my friends and acquaintances who used them, for the burgeoning women's movement, for "sensitive" males, most academics, and all talk about art, including, finally, my wife's. I ordered steak and organ meats at restaurants when everyone else was eating pasta, and took to drinking my bourbon from a water glass without ice, just as my father had.

And I developed some murky, father-related need to go into business. Two close friends and I took a game we had invented for our own pleasure in stalking and outwitting each other in the New Hampshire woods—a kind of tag played with dye-pellet pistols—and turned it into a company. We called this company The National Survival Game. It made lots of money for all of us, and then cost two of us the friendship of the third.

Next I began a company to warehouse all the imaginative possibilities I now wanted for myself: a sporting travel company that would send high-end sports all over the world to fish, shoot, and adventure at destinations I would have to check out for them personally. I started running faster and farther—to New Zealand for two months a year, Chile, Belize, Costa Rica,

New Guinea. I gave up writing entirely except for an occasional magazine article and a travel diary I kept for no better reason than to remind me what fly a particular fish had eaten at a particular time.

Most of the people who had crowded into our house and family garden just a few years before were gone by now. Only a housekeeper and Patricia, whom I saw infrequently, between unpacking and packing again, were in the house regularly. And the garden was empty, its blooms untended, its fountain dry, its walls crumbling.

If I saw Patricia rarely, I couldn't seem to see her work at all—the new bright anger in it, the ragged loneliness, the despair that whistled through those big, strange, heartbroken pictures seemed to me just so much modern chiaroscuro. She was as desperately caught up in her painting as I was in travel, and I resented all the time she spent at it and even believed her to be somehow painting against me. I would stalk down the hill from the house to her studio in the barn around eight at night in a mindless fury and ask if she planned to help me make some dinner or if she just wanted me to make it and bring it down to her on a goddamned platter.

"I don't care what you do," she would say, without turning away from her easel.

She was seeing a psychiatrist and I didn't want to hear about that, let alone her "issues," so we simply stopped talking much. One day while she was at the psychiatrist's office, I went into the hostile territory of her studio to look for paper towels, and found instead a packet of letters. They were from a young Southern man who some time before had sent me a short story to read. I had never gotten around to the story, but Patricia had read it, liked it, and had written the man to tell him so. Out of that note had grown a year-long correspondence—almost fifty letters from him, each warmer and more intimate than the one before. It was clear from those letters that the man and Patricia had exchanged photographs but had not yet met. It was also clear that he didn't intend to keep the relationship purely epistolary for much longer: His most recent letters nearly vibrated with growing intention, and in the last of them he had invited Patricia to meet him in Atlantic City. I sat on the stool in Patricia's studio, surrounded by big, vivid pictures of her unhappiness, and read every one of the letters. It nearly broke my heart trying to imagine what wording of loneliness and longing from my wife could have prompted such a fervor of sympathy from this young man who had never met her, such a passionate desire to comfort her.

When I finished reading it was almost dark in the studio. I sat there and waited for Patricia to return. I had no idea what to say to her. I thought I wanted to be understanding and loving, but I was not and neither was she. We were bitter, furious animals over those letters. I threw them at her, knocking over a jar of red paint; she kicked in a door; and I went up to the house alone. That night our dream house—the place we had been working toward ever since the undergraduate apartment in Alabama—became the first house where Patricia and I ever slept apart out of anger.

My father died in March of 1988, while I was between trips to New Zealand. He had been sick for a number of years and was eighty-two years old, but still so indomitable and in control of his life that his death astonished everyone who knew him. For the past ten years he and I had been careful friends, enjoying each other's company on fishing and hunting trips and avoiding the anger buttons both of us knew how to push. And we had traveled far enough together down the narrow, stony road of our relationship without either of us quitting it to have developed real respect and fondness for each other. But secretly, I think, we both couldn't help waiting for the other shoe to drop: he for me to go back to being an unaccountable, semi-criminal teenager; me for a return of the bewildering, shaming censoriousness of his drinking years. A year before he died he lay propped up by pillows in his huge bed, watching the squirrels on the bird feeder outside with no intention of ever shooting one again, and told me I was a fool to stop writing for the sporting travel business—for any business, in fact.

"You never wanted me to be a writer," I reminded him. "You wanted me to be a businessman."

"That was then." Even sick he had a grin that could light up a whole room, and he grinned it. "Now I want you to go back to being who you are and quit screwing around."

So when he died, true to the history of our relationship, I took most of the money he left me and put it against the red ink of my travel business, ultimately making more red ink. It may be that a man, as the saying goes, can only really become his own man when his father dies, but in my case the reaction was delayed.

The next year I was invited to fish on the first U.S. team to compete, with twenty other countries, in the annual World Fly-Fishing Championships. The competition that year was in Tasmania, and after it, I figured I might as well take three weeks to explore the wilderness light-tackle fishing on the remote northeast coast of Australia.

Patricia didn't want me to go on this trip. I was scheduled to leave on Thanksgiving Day and to return two days before Christmas, meaning I'd miss, for the first time ever, a big part of the kids' winter vacation. Also, she said, we badly needed some time together alone. "I need you not to go on this trip," she said in our bed one morning; there was snow falling. "Please don't go." I told her not to be silly, told her it was business, and got out of bed. A few days later we had a dismal Thanksgiving dinner at a friend's house, and I left before dessert to fly off for Tasmania.

A week later, when the competition was over, I called Patricia from a red-wood phone booth at the edge of a sheep meadow. I was supposed to go fishing in ten minutes with the pretty wife of the ex–prime minister of Australia and I wanted the phone conversation to go well and quickly. It didn't. It was nearly midnight back in New Hampshire and Patricia was in bed.

"I want you to come home. Now," she said.

"I can't. You know I'm going up north to . . ."

"Come home *now*, you sonofabitch!" she screamed into the phone.

"Is Ro [our live-in housekeeper] there? Quit yelling, for God's sake. I'll be home in three weeks—this is my *job.*"

There was a long, long silence. I was looking at the ragged rear end of an old Tasmanian ewe, marked in blue by the belly of a ram that had recently bred her. Right after Patricia and I married, when I was lifting weights and big as a house, I broke a long-standing record at a restaurant called the Catfish King by eating twenty-two chicken breasts and all the slaw and hush puppies that went with them. Breaking the record won me not having to pay for the meal. It also caused Patricia, who was pregnant, to throw up in the restaurant's ladies room, and me to do the same after we got home. I didn't know this then, but I know it now: Anything you want in life is available, even free, if you have appetite enough for it. And the other side of that coin is that big appetites can make you and the people around you sick. Staring at the old ewe's butt, I had a sudden vision of a very late night, movie-opening party Patricia and I had been to a few months before in New York. I was sitting in a chair in someone's suite at the Carlyle Hotel and straddling my lap was the voracious wife of one of my best friends. We were twined up appealingly in each other, this lady and I, and she was blowing an animal tranquilizer called PCP into my nose with a straw, when Patricia walked in from one of the suite's other rooms. Patricia had on a white dress that made her look like a little girl. She stood in the doorway staring at me in the same way she had in the Catfish King just before she got sick.

Waiting in a red-wood phone booth in Tasmania for Patricia to shriek something else into the phone from our bed, I felt suddenly stuffed to the gills and nauseated with my life, and sick in my bones for home—not the house I was connected to by thousands of miles of wire, but someplace I didn't even know how to find anymore.

She didn't shriek. She said, very steadily and quietly, "Charles, I want a divorce."

The following June I took Latham, Greta, and Shelby to Montana for two weeks. We spent the first five days camping out on a float trip down through the spectacular Smith River

canyon and then a week fishing out of the town of Twin
Bridges. We had been planning this trip for over a year. Two
of my oldest friends from Alabama joined us for the float trip.
Our outfitter and guides were good friends, too, men I love
fishing and being with. We had beautiful weather, good food
and drink, and great fishing and company in gorgeous country
for two weeks. It was a dream trip, a perfect trip—and my kids
and I held each other's spilling guts in throughout it and tried
to smile now and then.

Calmly, Patricia had told me when I got back from my
month in Australia that she was going to New York for the rest
of the winter to paint and live in a friend's apartment: She
wanted to get her career moving again and felt she had to be in
New York to do that. About us, she said, we would see how we
both felt in the spring.

I spent the winter alone with my two dogs in the house in
New Hampshire, trying to become a different person. That
becoming began with guilt and a self-loathing that was as bitter
as the bile that comes up in your throat after vomiting. I worked
selling sporting travel during the day, came home, drank, made
myself a meal I usually didn't eat, and began asking the house
and the dogs how I could've gotten to where I found myself—
bottomed out, with everything I cared about at risks that I had
put it to. I would wander around the house bellowing accusa-
tions at myself. "What was I thinking?" I'd shout at Fields or
Arthur. "*Nooo*, I can't come home when you need me to or to
be with the kids on their vacation—I've got to go to northern
fucking *Australia* to fish for *barramundi* . . ."

For two and a half months I went nowhere but to work,
and I saw and talked to no one I didn't have to see or talk to.

For exercise, I would go walking out on the frozen, snow-covered expanse of Lake Sunapee to let the wind bore into me like a dentist's drill, to let it take my breath and deaden me. In my empty house I took the phone off the hook, pulled my guilt around me like an old, ugly shawl against the iron New Hampshire cold, and babbled self-hatred to myself and my dogs. And when I went to bed each night I met there exactly the same suffocating, chaotic panic I had felt throughout the ocean storm of my adolescence. I understood clearly that I had years ago, miraculously, found all the refuge from storms I would ever need in the garden of Patricia and my family and that, unaccountably, I had let that garden go to ruin and then walked out of it. Toward dawn, exhausted from crawling around in the sided hail looking for a way back in that I knew I couldn't find, I would sometimes go to sleep.

Then, in March, my hopelessness and self-pity broke like a fever. I went corn-snow skiing on the mountain near my house and knew I could find my way back to myself and my family if Patricia would let me. I called her and told her I felt like I'd walked out of a long tunnel, like I'd had a heart transplant, that I wanted nothing but to change and to start over with her however and wherever she wanted.

She would meet me in Washington, D.C., in late May for Greta's graduation from Georgetown, she said. We would talk about all that then.

On Easter Sunday I went to communion and, amid the lilies and the Christian sacraments of rebirth and death's defeat, of sorrow and catastrophe redeemed into joy, forgiveness, and love, I thanked God for my long, dark winter of suffering and for my emergence from it. I traced the shape of a lily on a prayer book with my finger. I took the bread of heaven and the cup of salvation, the holy food and drink of thanksgiving, and felt myself to be a revenant that Easter Sunday, a barely saved revenant. I thanked God for that and prayed Patricia would let me begin to show her in Washington what I had returned to.

She would not. When the kids and I walked into the apartment where we were all staying for the graduation week-end, she was already there, thin, pale, doing Oriental-looking calming exercises on the floor. As soon as we put down our bags, she asked the kids to go take a walk. When they left, she faced me, her hands on her hips, standing in front of a big window overlooking a courtyard eight floors below. She was shockingly different. She was willowy and haunted-looking, and there was a gauntly erotic look about her—a grasping, predatory need in her eyes that scared the hell out of me. I wanted to hold and stroke her for a solid month and put the contentment back in her face; I also wanted to haul her down to the floor and make love to her. Looking me in the eye this time, she told me again that she wanted a divorce and that nothing I could possibly say or do would change her mind. There was no mistaking that she meant it. And then, for a long couple of minutes, all I wanted to do was run past her and dive out the window at her back.

I started pacing around the apartment—for some reason picking up objects off tables, looking at them without register-ing what they were, and putting them down again—panicked and ranting about how I had changed, would change. It was too late for that, she said, looking at me behind the hard, sexy, unknowable mask of her new life. "You don't even know what you've done to me," she said and laughed.

Somehow the rest of that day passed after Patricia told Greta, Latham, and Shelby that she was going to get a divorce.

And somehow we made it through a Vietnamese dinner that night with one of Greta's roommates and her divorced father, though we all must have seemed like zombies to the father and the girl. Patricia and I had to share a bed that night and the next—two sweltering nights in an unair-conditioned apartment. We lay side by side but miles apart in the hot dark, talking about ourselves in the past tense, in a lockstep, hopeless dialogue.

On Sunday, after speaker Michael Dorris had welcomed the new Georgetown graduates to "the fray, the battle of life," we watched our daughter, Greta, receive her diploma in an outdoors ceremony, then fly across the grass to hug and kiss her friends, her long yellow hair bobbing under her mortarboard, her vivid face insisting on the joy of this day over its pain. In a photograph someone took of the five of us after the graduation, it is hard to tell we were no longer a family: Everyone is smiling except Patricia, and if you didn't know her, you might just think this wife, this mother, always looked stabbed in the heart.

After the two most agonizing days of any of our lives, Patricia and I went back to New Hampshire with Latham, Greta, and Shelby, who treated us gently and watchfully, as if we were terminally ill. Patricia stayed there for a week, wandering around, telling the place good-bye silently, and packing her clothes. She demanded that the kids and I go ahead on the trip to Montana that all of us had planned to go on. She wanted to come back to New Hampshire from New York while we were gone, she said, to be alone in the house and get the rest of her things. She would talk to me in a month or two, whenever she figured out about the lawyers and all that.

Her beautiful face, animated day and night for as long as

I had known her by a flowerlike, open sweetness, was now closed, distracted, and bitter. She slept in our bed but wouldn't let me touch her. When the kids and I left for the airport, she told me, "Get a new life. I am."

With my two friends from Alabama there were six of us on the float trip down the Smith River, plus the outfitters and guides. We floated and fished the breathtaking canyon-locked wilderness river during the day and camped in tents along its banks at night. In Bob Butler and Tom Montgomery we had with us two of the best fly-fishing guides in the Rocky Mountain west, but my true guides through the winding, canyoned despair of that river trip and the following week were Latham, Greta, and Shelby.

In so many ways our children are our guides. They can and will lead us to the purest love there is, the purest self-sacrifice, the purest joy in being human, the purest rewards for labor. And in the act of parenting, our children are guides to the individual secrets of their personalities. They will lead us to those secrets if we follow carefully, and those secrets can open the fist of parenting, make it an easy act of friendship. And there is something else: The secrets of our children's personalities, those bright treasures picked up on the guided hunt of their childhoods, can sometimes save our skins.

There is a Grimms Brothers fairy story about a tailor and a shoemaker who meet on a road and decide to travel together to a great city where they hope to get work. The tailor is a cheerful, optimistic, life-loving sort, while the shoemaker is scheming and stoic. They come to a V in the road: One way leads to the city in seven days, the other in only two. The travelers choose one of the roads without knowing which it is. The tailor, who gets through life on luck and God's good will, packs for a two-day trip. The shoemaker has found that a man can count only on caution and planning; he packs for seven days. As it turns out, they have chosen the seven-day road and the tailor is made to suffer on the journey for his insouciance. But later in the story he is redeemed by his open, trusting spirit, and the shoemaker, who fared well on the journey, is made to suffer for his scheming. We are all, the story implies, either two- or seven-day packers and we go through life harvesting the consequences, both good and bad, of being one or the other.

Latham, our oldest child, is a charmed and brilliant two-day packer—a natural athlete with an actor's good looks and a body so strong, graceful, and competent that it has never occurred to him that he might need anything more than it to get to the city. He is quiet, mordant, idiosyncratic, witty, and good with his hands. He will work hard if the work makes sense to him, and not work at all if it doesn't, but creative play is his real métier. He skis, windsurfs, and snow-boards well enough to make a living at those things, and he acts, sings, plays the guitar, and makes visual art. He is a kind, stubborn dreamer who dislikes clutching and combat and who never pushes or pulls at life but uses its own momentum, like a judo master, to position it. He believes that laissez-faire is more, and he has more elusive and effortless glide to his life than anyone I have ever known.

Like Latham, his adored older brother, and like his mother, Shelby is also a two-day packer, who needs only his music and his sense of justice to get to the city. He was born being very old, with a rigorous sense of fairness that makes his nickname, Judge, uncannily correct for him. All his life he has had a grave self-possession and a quietly happy calm at the center of his personality that have made people love him and seek his company. Perhaps because of his great feeling for music, he listens better than anyone I know. He plays a number of instruments expertly, sings, arranges, and composes. He is tall and thin, with a sharply angled face that can seem a little tragic in repose. He can remind you of some animal with a sound, self-sufficient, good-humored life, and his sister believes he is disturbingly Christlike.

That sister, Greta, is as much a seven-day packer as I am, and would buy a ten-day pack if she could find one, to better carry around all her well-arranged enthusiasms. Blond-haired and blue-eyed like her mother and brothers, she has a high-spirited, blowsy, wild horse sort of beauty that is unself-conscious and barely tended. She is, and always has been, busy: She is a professional singer and songwriter; a snow-boarder, mountain climber, and fly-fisher; a playwright, photographer, and actress. She has more close friends than most people have acquaintances, and a fierce, mothering love for the people closest to her. She is a little unbelievable, Greta is, but so absolutely unaffected and direct that she has always had the jump on any envy coming her way. She believes in living hard and efficiently, with passion and solid plans. Occasionally she will outrun her lungs and a locked-in-the-basement frailty can show its face. Then she goes fearless. She is a long-distance runner with a sprinter's legs and a lioness's heart.

All three of our children learned when they were small how to keep hiking on blisters. They learned how to keep each other's spirits up on a pack trip after eight hours in the saddle when the guide is lost—and how to paddle into a stiff wind and not quit paddling until they got to where they were going. All three of them know how to stick things out, and they will make it to the city by any road you put them on.

For five days on the Smith River and then for a week in a log cabin in Twin Bridges these three people, whom for years I had done my best to guide, guided me. On the river, surrounded by other people, we could not talk to each other about what I had caused to happen to us, and not talking about it felt to me like death. Latham, Greta, and Shelby showed me how to get through that. I watched them, knowing the blisters they were hiking on were as painful as mine, and did what they did.

Our first night alone together in Twin Bridges I drove them over to a restaurant in Ennis for dinner, and on that drive—because I thought knowing would be better for them than guessing—I told them exactly how I had failed at the one thing in life I had most wanted to succeed at. I told them how I had ignored and bullied Patricia for the past few years without even realizing I was doing it: how I had quit listening to her, smothered her priorities with mine, deserted her when she needed me, and been imperious and impatient with her. I told them she had done nothing to me to deserve all that mistreatment and, in fact, had never once in our life together been anything other than loyal and loving. And I said, meaning it, that I would happily lie down and be eaten alive by ants if I could take back what I had done and put us back as the whole family we had been.

Being eaten alive by ants wouldn't do that, of course, and I had no idea what would. Putting our family back together was the ultimate Survival Situation for me, though—I did know

that. I was on a deserted island and had let the boat that brought
me there rot and sink out of inattention; I was in an airplane I
couldn't fly without a copilot and had pushed the copilot out
of the plane . . . What does this man do now? was the question
before me and my children.

One of them, the angriest at me, at first said, "It's his
Situation, let him solve it." "No it's not. It's all of ours," said
the other two. And over the course of the week, in fishing boats
and restaurants, driving places and during late-night talks in the
cabin, their personalities guided me to a few skin-saving an-
swers. Latham's said: Give it up if you want to get it back. Get
your life going again on a new track, said Greta's, give her
something more than words to come back to. And Shelby's said:
Be quiet; listen; love. All three of them told me: Stick it out,
don't even think about quitting, ever. And all three of them said:
Be there and be ready if she needs you.

And later that month Patricia did come to need me. By
then she was no longer seeing friends in the city or going out
to parties and the theater. She was holed up in her borrowed
West Side apartment, painting as if her life depended on it and
talking to herself. She was twenty pounds lighter than when she
had first come to New York, not sleeping at night, and breaking
into tears on the street every time she saw a couple who looked
happy. She had begun to feel stormed by New York—by the
man who exposed himself to her on the street, by the busboy
pickets surrounding Tavern on the Green, a restaurant just
outside her window, who shouted and beat on trash cans
twenty-four hours a day, by the swinish gallery owner who
propositioned her before looking at her slides. She awoke every
morning to the pickets and her heartbeat, feeling marauded,

defenseless, and deserted. (In the previous two years both her father and mine had died, and my sister's husband, our beloved Don Burke, was near death from colon cancer.)

It was Patricia's time to bottom out. She walked out onto Central Park West one morning and gave away a diamond pin to the first female beggar she met. Over the next few days she gave away to astonished panhandlers silver bracelets and necklaces, a gold watch, a diamond and ruby ring, a pearl necklace, a pair of diamond clips, and, finally, her engagement and wedding rings. Every piece of jewelry she owned. A thorough arson.

"For all Thy blessings, known and unknown, remembered and forgotten, we give Thee thanks," goes an old prayer of thanksgiving for grace, that silver, life-giving shower that falls into our lives now and then out of a clear sky. After she gave away her wedding ring Patricia went back to the apartment, wet from a sudden rain of grace, and could cry for the loss of that ring and all it represented. For the first time, she could want her family back.

Half-crazy with grief and loss, hollow-eyed and numb, she came home at the end of July needing me, and I was there and ready to be quiet, to listen and to love, and to show her that she could stay and learn to count on me again. For the first few weeks she was like an invalid. I cooked her meals and brought them to her in bed—on a platter. I rubbed her back, took her for short walks in the woods, and read her to sleep at night. Whenever Patricia was most unhappy and frightened as a child, she would get into bed with her minister father and fall asleep by stroking his closed eyelids with her fingertips. That particular touch gave her the consolation and hope of trust. One morning toward the end of August, I awoke with her fingertips on my eyelids, where she had left them when she fell asleep, and where they had not been for years.

The long storm was finally over, because we both wanted and trusted it to be, and even though there was wreckage everywhere, we had insurance—the good hands of nearly thirty years of marriage, our children, and a history of not being beaten—that paid for starting over. We began going to a wonderful female counselor named Rhea. I read books I had never thought I'd read, on the nature of permanent love, on roads less traveled, and on the psychology of relationships. We spent an hour every day walking and talking, and we discovered that forgetting is the best forgiveness.

I sold my travel business. Everywhere Patricia or I went, we went together and with our kids, as we used to do. And we began dreaming of a new landscape and way of life in which we could begin again what we had begun years ago—in which we could, as a family, get back to simplicity and purity of purpose, and perhaps recapture an old dream for ourselves and our lives together.

That old skinflint Thoreau tells us,

> It is desirable that a man be clad so simply that he can lay his hands on himself in the dark, and that he live in all respects so compactly and preparedly that, if an enemy take the town, he can, like the old philosopher, walk out the gate empty-handed without anxiety.

During the fall and winter, as Patricia and I grew back into each other and found that we had more delight to give each other than we had ever known we had, we both began to imagine a more compact life in a place that housed dreams rather than incorporating them and from which, if an enemy were to take the town, we had only to gather up those dreams and each other in order to leave whole. We imagined some simple, easily managed, beautiful place where we could come to live in and through each other and our children again, a place where we could replant our family garden and rebuild the walls and gate.

And we decided that we wanted the home for this new beginning and these new/old dreams to be a house we would build with our own hands.

5

According to writer Tracy Kidder, house building is "both an act of memory and also a fresh start." In his wonderful book *House*, Mr. Kidder points out that for the New World Puritan building a house was an act of religious transfiguration, a godly act creating an imitation of godly handiwork in which the hearth was the heart, the rafters the bones, the clapboards skin, the roof the head, the windows eyes, and the door a mouth. " 'Housebuilding,' " Mr. Kidder quotes folklorist Robert St. George, "was conceived as an heroic effort to stop time, suspend decay and interrupt the ordained flow to ruin that started with Adam's fall.' " And he further quotes Mircea Eliade, the great anthropologist of religions, who calls home construction " 'a new organization of the world and life.' "

In fact, until you do it yourself it is hard to imagine how godlike and exhilarating it does feel to begin from scratch with hands and tools to build a house to shelter yourself and your family—particularly when scratch means nothing but canvas between you and the weather.

The reorganization of our world and life, our heroic effort

to stop time and suspend decay, our fresh start and act of memory and religious transfiguration, commenced with some urgency in knee-deep mud on the day after the monster storm hit us. The weather on this day was crisp and beautiful and everyone was elated. We had not been blown away, and now, here we were, our tents reinforced, but with no house, and no way of having one again until we built one. The feeling that came from acknowledging that fact was sharp both with liberation and challenge, and all of us took it with us to our first day's work on the cabin.

We began that work by building the two floor-joist "boxes" that, when set atop the cabin's foundation piers of railroad ties that we'd sunk into the ground, would form the substructure of the floor. Omere and Rob had bought and stocked tool belts for the rest of us. I strapped mine on after breakfast, then adjusted it to ride a little lower, in Omere's gunslinger style. There was a big twenty-two-ounce framing hammer hanging from a leather noose. Also hanging from the belt or stuck into nifty little pouches and loops were a cat's-paw for pulling nails, a chalk line and measuring tape, a triangular level, an Exacto knife, a chisel, a thick pencil, and a metal nail punch. Omere had even filled the belt's nail pockets with big galvanized deck nails. As I followed him and Rob, Latham, Shelby, and Nick over to the tarp-covered pile of lumber and watched them deftly pull out long two by ten spruce boards, cocking them on end and sighting along them for straightness, I suddenly had a bleak vision of myself as one of the pathetic fly-fishermen I run into all the time who are tricked out with all the best and newest gear but don't know how to cast.

"Are you a fan or a player here?" Latham asked me with a grin.

I picked up a board and looked down it.

In midmorning Tom Mattie's wife, Mary, brought us some rolls. A little later, Heather DeCoste, the wife of Ralph's brother, Andy, came up with two pies. And in the early afternoon a young fisherman named Jody Beshong drove up in a Jeep and said he was there to take our orders for lobster—how many would we like off his boat when he came in from pulling traps the next day?

After lunch on the blueberry shack deck Patricia and Greta strapped on their work belts, too, and helped finish building the boxes. Omere and Rob cut the boards and the rest of us nailed them together, at various levels of proficiency. When I noticed that Latham and Shelby were driving their nails with fewer than half the blows I was using, I copied their longer swings and . . . bent a lot of nails. After the boxes had been assembled on the ground we lifted them up onto the railroad ties, leveled them, gang-nailed them to each other, and anchored them to the foundation with steel gussets. Then we nailed and glued sheets of three-quarter-inch tongue-in-groove plywood over them and, by late afternoon, we had the finished floor of our cabin.

Latham, Shelby, and I shaved and bathed in the beaver pond down the road, got the truck stuck in the mud, and walked back to the camp. Then Patricia and I took chairs over and sat with Arthur and Fields on the new first floor of the cabin to watch the sun drop toward the bay.

We had just seated ourselves when someone shouted "Hello!" from out on the cape, and a small, grizzled man appeared, striding quickly toward us through the waist-high brush. He walked up with a big snaggletoothed grin, handed Patricia a little bouquet of wildflowers, and hoisted himself up to sit on the edge of our platform. He looked out at Cape

George and scratched Fields's yellow head. "Beautiful evening," he said.

We agreed and introduced ourselves.

"Uh huh."

". . . and you are?" I asked.

"They call me 'Bill the Rambler' because I love to walk. I walk all over these woods and cliffs. I just walked up here now from Linwood," he said, referring to the little harbor to the east of us. "I have a trailer down there, but I spend all day walking—in the woods, mostly, finding things to eat."

"To eat?"

"Oh my, yes—there's Indian pear and wild grape, raspberry and blueberry, blackberry, cranberry, wild strawberry, wild apples in the fall. Any amount of things to eat in these woods. . . . Tell me this, Mister," he said, looking up at me. "Do you like to see knives thrown?"

"Sure," I said. Patricia glanced at me.

"Well, I was a knife thrower, you know. In the Canadian Special Forces. We captured the town of Monte Cassino over there in Italy by climbing those bloody cliffs with our faces painted black while the Germans were asleep. We took out their sentries with throwing knives and those men never made a sound. I could bring a few of my knives up here sometime. I throw hatchets too."

Bill looked to be under sixty but was seventy-two, he said. He was as hard and knotty as a scrub alder, with a silver crew cut, a week's beard, and four or five teeth to his name. He seemed serene and intense at the same time, with a lantern jaw and a good humor that was somehow predatory.

"Those your kids?" he asked, looking over at the deck

where Greta, Latham, and Shelby were getting supper ready and
Nick was playing the guitar.

"Three of them," I said. For some reason I was a little
alarmed by the question.

"My kids are all over everywhere," he said. He made a
series of throwing gestures as if he were throwing rocks into a
pond. "Scattered like the pellets from a shotgun."

The evening was cold, with a rising new moon. We sat for
a couple of minutes in silence watching the sun go down, the
green light at the entrance to Tracadie Harbor, and the slate-
blue sea. Then Bill the Rambler slid off the floor of the cabin
and walked off toward the cape. Seen from the back, walking,
he could have been a twenty-year-old man.

"Come back sometime," said Patricia tentatively.

"Maybe," he said, turning and waving, "I never know
where I'm going to ramble."

That night I had dreams with knives and storms in them
and I woke early with a new full-blown sense of jeopardy and
a nervous urgency to get the cabin finished as quickly as possible. Until the cabin was done there would be not only storms
and lightning to worry about, but power saws and drills, hard
to read electrical cords running from the generator, leaking
propane, falling things—a host of unforeseeable threats, like a
covey of invisibly thrown knives in the air.

Wanting to make the most of the two weeks that Omere
had left to help us and the wonderful, cool, bright weather that
followed the storm, I began to push myself and everybody else.
I rose at six every morning to square the camp and make coffee.

Omere would drive up from the DeCostes' shack on the bluff around seven and he and I would have breakfast and plan out the day. The others would turn out by seven thirty and we'd all be working by eight—Omere, Rob, Latham, Shelby, and Nick on the cabin, and Patricia and Greta at cleaning the tents, making grocery lists, heating water to wash dishes and clothes, and making lunch. In the afternoons Patricia and Greta would either help with the work on the cabin or go grocery shopping in Antigonish.

I had promised the kids we would take some time off each afternoon to play and enjoy the place, but the week after the storm I kept them working every day until six thirty or seven. I worked alongside them on the cabin. I also juggled money and worried about running out of it, bought and ordered building supplies, planned with Omere, and shopped and cooked with Patricia and Greta. I shaved and washed every evening in cold pond water, tried to ignore the growing pain in my hips even though it kept me from sleeping, and fell into my sleeping bag each night around midnight—after closing down the camp, snuffing the bonfires, and making certain all the gas lanterns were out—in an exhausted, increasingly wrongheaded blur.

With what little free time they had, Latham, Shelby, and Nick had begun to build a skateboarding "half-pipe" ramp in the woods behind their tent. For no very good reason, both the ramp they were building and the time and money (both theirs) they were spending on it irritated me. Made out of God's own amount of raw plywood and dished up at either end to a height of about five feet, the huge, ugly structure looked like it belonged in a city park, not a spruce grove. And all that energy going into building it and then sliding up and down it, I grumbled to Patricia in Thoreauvian snits, should be going into the cabin.

I grew equally irritable over the time stolen from building by a steady, generous stream of visiting neighbors. On our two previous trips to the property, Patricia and I had gotten to know a few people in the community: Walter and Edna Boudreau, the stately, ironic, tough old couple we had bought the land from; their grandson, Shawn, and his wife, Gabriella; gentle Tom Mattie and his wife, Mary; Ralph and Maria DeCoste and their six kids; Ralph's brother, Andy, and his wife, Heather; Michael and Anne Delorey from the bottom of our road. And we had met more since we had arrived—quite a few more, since dozens of people had come up the shale road out of curiosity and neighborliness to introduce themselves and bring rolls and pies, lobsters, good wishes and welcomes, and, during and just after the storm, to offer us the use of their homes. There was the lobsterman, Jody Beshong, and his brother, Reggie, with the four-wheeler; the Andrews family, Tory and Judy, and their kids, Nicole, Amanda, Dave, and John, another four-wheeler who came up every day at least once; Ron and Sue; Lloyd and Debbie; sweet Lorraine Mattie, Tom and Mary's daughter; big Glenn Bears; Vern the carpenter; Dave Clark the telephone man and salmon fisherman; Bill the Rambler; Eugene the plumber and his wife Eleanor . . .

By the time the storm hit it seemed we had met practically everyone in the community, and by the time it was over it was clear that many of them had become our friends. They smiled at us when they talked about the storm, and Tom Mattie called Patricia the toughest woman north of Bangor. They came up at all times of the day and night and stayed awhile, drinking a

Keiths beer or two at the picnic table, their children on their knees or running through the growing frame of the cabin. They brought with them a totally open, uninhibited hospitality that none of us were used to, coming as we did from standoffish New England, and though we were grateful for it and often delighted by it, it made us all a little uneasy from time to time. Occasionally the kids felt studied, as though our neighbors were amateur anthropologists with an interest in American subspecies. Patricia sometimes minded the unscheduled and regular losses of privacy, at meals particularly. And I, in my mounting rush to finish the cabin, began to see every daytime visit as a lost or interrupted half hour of whip cracking.

As I was to learn, nervous haste has no place in building and is the nemesis of the amateur carpenter. Central to good carpentry is the discipline of thinking ahead patiently and clearly; of "seeing the end in the beginning," as Tracy Kidder puts it; of measuring twice and cutting once. Building a house, even a small one, is a painstaking form of ordering, and certain laws govern it that cannot be shortcut: Things have to be level, so a tennis ball won't roll from one side of your floor to the other; things have to join to a sixteenth of an inch, to be parallel.

What you don't really know until you do it is that building a house is not a single large job, but hundreds of little ones, each of which has to be done correctly for the next to be done correctly and for the whole to come square. Impatience simply leads to mistakes and waste, to what carpenters call "cobby work," to measuring once and cutting twice. The tempo of any construction is set by the synapses between concept and execution—you plan, then you do; plan, then do; replan, then do; redo; plan, then do—and effectively fast builders, builders who are fast without hurrying, are people with the experience and talent to execute one step correctly as they are conceiving the next.

Happily for me I had two such people in Omere and Rob, and the cabin came along quickly and well despite my agitations. Whenever I started rushing, Rob or Omere would give me a little piece of nonessential work to do, let me botch it up, and then—in the time-honored convention of carpenters everywhere—invite me to write my name on the mistake.

Only five days after the storm we had the indoor outhouse installed, the frames of all four walls standing, and the rafter trusses built and stacked against the walls. The cabin had come to look like a cabin, and there was an astonishing thrill in looking at its bare bones framed by the sea, and in standing inside it and seeing the landscape through our own created openings, our own developing geometry. The evening before the rafters went up Patricia and I got down on our hands and knees with tapes and drew out the interior of the cabin on the floor—drawing the bed to scale where it would go, the wood stove, the refrigerator and kitchen cabinets, the walls and door of the bathroom. Fields and Arthur followed us around, nosing us and wondering what was up, as Patricia and I crawled over the floor, delightedly playing house.

The next morning I got everyone working even earlier than usual, and in one long, exhausting day we raised the rafters, strapped them, and built the sleeping loft. At the end of the day we nailed a spruce bough to the roof's ridge line, as builders have done for hundreds of years, to propitiate the tree gods. Then, just at dusk, we all stepped back and looked at the completed skeleton of our cabin.

In all building traditions, writes Tracy Kidder, "the roof represents the essential element of shelter, and once the frame of a roof exists the shape of a building comes clear." Our roof pitched forty-five degrees for fourteen feet to the north; to the south it pitched at the same angle and distance to an eleven-foot shed roof that was fifteen degrees steep. It was a sail-like, elegant roofline, one commonly used in Nova Scotia in the nineteenth century for barns with attached sheds. Many of those old buildings, their cedar shingles silvery with age, are still standing in our part of the province, and Patricia and Omere and I had wanted the cabin to have something of their solid, oceangoing shapeliness. So we adopted the roofline of these last-century barn/sheds and hoped for the best. Stepping back now and looking at the cabin's finished shape, we saw that we had precisely what we had wanted: The little, framed building seemed to be on tack against the darkening bay.

We were all tired. We had just finished a supper of smoked turkey and garlic mashed potatoes, and Latham and Shelby went over to start the bonfire. It had showered off and on through the afternoon. The branches and twigs we used for kindling were wet, so Latham put a big pile of them together in the center of the fire pit and doused it with gasoline from one of the ten-gallon plastic containers we used to fill the generator. This is not a good fire-starting practice, as any handbook on camping safety will tell you in bold print, but we had slid into using it when our bonfire wood was wet—dribbling gas out of the small air hole of the container over a pile of kindling, then stepping well away and throwing a match onto the twigs. This night, as I say, everyone was tired, and Shelby threw a match into the kindling while Latham was still pouring gasoline.

The rest of us were talking thirty feet away at the big picnic table on the deck. We heard the whoosh of the igniting gasoline, and looked up to see Latham spinning around, flames all around his feet and legs and a lariat of fire around his waist. When the gas ignited, a rope of flame had run from the twigs up the stream of poured gas to the container's air hole. Latham was trying to put it out by spinning around with the container, but gas was still spilling and burning in a circle around his midsection. Fields, our golden retriever, shot off the deck for his adored Latham and actually tried to wrestle the gas container away from him. Rob was the quickest human: He snatched up a canvas tarp that was rolled under one of the serving counters and threw it over the gas container that Latham had finally tossed when flames started running up his arms.

Latham had only a few singed hairs on his arms and Fields a few singed whiskers. But not one of us even had to look at the tarp-extinguished gas container lying where it had landed two feet from the generator to realize how close we had come to disaster.

The next morning Latham walked up to breakfast in a full scowl. He had grown a Fu Manchu mustache, and it and his bad mood made him look a little like a Kurosawa warlord. It had nothing to do with the accident the night before, he said, but he wasn't working today: He hadn't come to Canada to be a slave; the schedule I had them on was ridiculous, and he was taking the day off. He poured himself a bowl of cereal, sat down, and glowered at me over it. Then Shelby and Nick came up

from the tent the boys shared and were more coolly mutinous.
Nick was going home the following day. He loved to fish for
bass and had brought some tackle with him when I told him I'd
take him bass fishing in the Annapolis Valley. He hadn't been
near the valley, or a bass pond anywhere else, and he had worked
as hard as any of us, in pain much of the time from an old back
injury.

"You guys don't want to work today either, huh?" I asked
them.

"Nope," said Shelby quietly. "We're going to see if we can
find Nick a bass and then skate on the ramp this afternoon."

I should have said "Fine"; I should have said "Great!" and
congratulated them on that good plan and helped them get their
tackle together, but I said, "No, you're not. We only have
Omere for nine more days. There's no wind today and I want
to start the roofing." This was a mistake, and we went to war
then on the eating deck. It was a war I knew I shouldn't go to
and couldn't win, but I couldn't stop myself. And, as usual, I
went too far.

"I'd like to burn that goddamn half-pipe ramp," I told
them. (In fact, I was proud of it.) "If all you want to do is
skateboard like ten-year-olds, you don't belong up here anyway."

Latham stood up at that, his face showing I had hurt him.
He rinsed out his bowl and stalked off the deck. Shelby and
Nick followed him.

"Have a great time, guys," I shouted at their backs. "Rob
and Omere and I'll get the roof up while you're fishing and
skateboarding—don't even think about it."

I went back to my tent like Achilles, to sulk—and to wish
I was going bass fishing with my boys and Nick. I flopped down

on the big double sleeping bag that Patricia and I slept in, and
Fields and Arthur nosed in through the mosquito netting to join
me. In a few minutes Patricia came into the tent, sat down beside
me, and began rubbing my back.

"That wasn't pretty, was it?" I said.

"No."

"They're spoiled little shits."

"They just need some time off. They'll be fine tonight."
She stopped rubbing my back and sat there quietly on the bag
for a moment. I could feel her deflating. "Don't ruin this for
them, Charles," she said.

Latham had given up a summer of making good money
teaching windsurfing to be there; Shelby had wanted to be
working and playing music in Boston; Greta had broken off a
string of singing gigs in Jackson Hole. I felt badly out of whack
in some way I didn't know how to fix. My hips hurt. I felt a
hundred years old and hateful. I also felt misunderstood.

"This is just a lot harder than I thought it was going to
be."

"I thought we were doing fine," Patricia said and her voice
sounded frightened. She was certainly doing fine—loving everything, even the toughest parts, just swinging along inside her
own sweet rhythms. I felt like everything else was running
over—temperaments, tempers, the scrutiny we were under, what
was expected of everyone, the budget.

"We're not doing fine when half our crew takes a day off,
for no reason, when we need to get the roof up."

"You know," she said, "you're acting a lot like your old
self—just pushing, pushing, pushing, running around yelling at
people like some Third World general. Everybody here is trying

as hard as they can . . ." She stopped and I turned over and looked at her. Patricia picks at her thumb when she is unhappy, and she was doing that: Her fingers were dirty and chapped. Her hair was dirty too and wrapped up in an old scarf. And her face, for the first time since we had started all this, was a little desperate.

"Those boys would lie down and let a truck run over them for you." She stood up. "Please don't ruin this for them," she said again and left the tent.

I lay there with an arm over either dog and tried to breathe with my stomach the way all the Oriental self-help books tell you to do in order to balance and calm yourself. That's always struck me as asking a lot from breathing—especially in my case, where balance and calm have always been as out of reach as growing red hair—but it never hurts to try. Lying there in the tent between my snoozing dogs, I could actually feel how my scheduling, list-making, compulsive, peremptory personality— my push-whatever-it-is-too-far-then-keep-pushing-it personal- ity—could be as maddeningly repetitive and insistent as six hours of bagpipe music to a whole genus of calm, balanced, unimperative organisms that included my wife and both my sons.

Balance! I have a badly flawed inner ear for enthusiasms, I thought. Ever since childhood I had been falling completely for things—lurching between obsessions, bowling people over and damaging myself. Some part of that lurching had cost me both my hips. Pushing too hard at weight lifting, I had torn up a knee, a shoulder, and my lower back. Trying to go at red-line from one place to another, I had lost toes, cut arteries, perma- nently severed nerves, and blown my marriage like a head gasket.

I had even given myself gum disease from overflossing. In that pathetic little fact, I thought, there had to be some message to live by, but I was damned if I could come up with it. All I could see was that much too often I measured once and then spent all day cutting. The belly breathing didn't help with that, or make me feel any better about my cobby work with Nick and my sons, or clear my fog of details and worry; but it may have put me to sleep.

On the day after Nick went back to Providence, two weeks after we had arrived in Nova Scotia, Tom and Mary Mattie threw a party at their house. It started around five in the afternoon and was still going strong at one in the morning when we left over Mary's protest that we were going to miss "lunch," a big meal of cold cuts and salad that she was just about to serve. Supper had been five or six hours before and the platters of fried chicken, as many boiled lobsters as you wanted, the casseroles, slaw, macaroni and potato salads, and fresh-baked rolls and pies had managed to hold us.

The Matties have seven grown children, six of whom, along with seven grandchildren, live literally within a stone's throw of each other and their parents. Two of their sons work with Tom in the excavating business, along with two of his brothers. With the Matties, as with many other families in this Acadian community, family forms the very framework of life. All of Tom and Mary's kids and grandkids were at their party, along with forty or so neighbors. Tom had rigged a tarp over his porch against a little light rain that had started falling after supper, and people stood or sat out there, slapping mosquitoes, holding children and beers, and talking. A group of fiddlers and guitar players set themselves up in the kitchen and began to play French and Scottish tunes, *ceilidh* music, and after a while guests were step dancing and waltzing in the living room and all over the leaky porch.

In the kitchen Tom crooked his finger at me. I pushed my way over to him and he poured me a drink of local moonshine out of a Captain Morgan rum bottle. The stuff is brewed everywhere in Canada to get around the country's staggering taxes on alcohol. All of it is effective and some of it is quite good, including what Tom had just poured. "Dancing oil," Tom said. His big, kind face was flushed. I asked him if he step danced and he said no, but Mary did. He looked out the window to the porch and pulled me over to see Mary step dancing out there with one of her sons. Her feet were flying expertly beneath her nearly still upper body, beating out the old Acadian rhythms. She looked up and saw Tom and me watching her and winked at her husband.

No one in our group had to work at having a wonderful time at Tom and Mary's party, except for Fields and Arthur, who endured it in the back of the truck. That day we had finished the difficult and dangerous job of roofing the cabin; I had made up with Nick before he left; and Shelby and Latham and I were back on good terms. On the evening after our fight I had gone down to watch them skateboard and told them both I was sorry for the way I had acted. As gracefully as they swooped the ramp, they pretended they had never given it a thought. Driving back up the hill to the camp the whole crew was happier and looser than it had been for days—everyone but me. With a bellyful of homemade hooch, I only seemed to be.

Omere dreamed that night that the cabin blew away in a storm.

"What?" I croaked at him over breakfast the next day. "It couldn't, could it?"

"No. But look, there's a machinist down in Linwood—I'm going to have him make up some hurricane plates to tie the boxes to the piers. It'll make us both sleep better."

I drove down and picked up the big steel plates after lunch and Omere and I bolted them in. "She won't go anywhere now," he said.

"I'm glad you thought of this—it's one less thing I might've come up with to worry about."

"Hey," said Omere. "Cosmic flow."

That afternoon, while Patricia and Greta went clamming down on the beach, the rest of us began siding the house in beautiful, honey-colored shiplap cedar boards. The great architect Louis Kahn liked to say that certain building materials want to become certain kinds of structures. Omere, Patricia, and I had known all along that cedar wanted to be our cabin, just as our site—our high, sea-struck, windy cape—wanted the sloop of a building we were putting there. Cedar was tough and native. It smelled as good as the balsamy woods behind us, and it would weather to the color of clouds with a little rain in them. The roof we had just put up to cap the siding was galvanized steel with a blue enamel finish that picked up the colors of the midmorning summer sky—and of the bay on a bright afternoon.

We wanted to incorporate our cabin into its place with the right choice of materials. We also wanted to incorporate the place into the materials of the cabin. Doing this has provided some builders with a ripe, magically reassuring pleasure ever since it was the only way to build. Thoreau, for example, was delighted to collect stones from the shore of Walden Pond for his chimney and to hew his studs, rafters, and timbers from "tall, arrowy white pines, still in their youth" that grew near his site. Patricia and I had already built a hearth for the wood stove out of mauve shale stones we had gathered on the beach, and that evening when I drove the truck down to the beach to pick up Patricia and Greta, we hauled back to the cabin with us a ten-foot driftwood log, about six inches in diameter, that Patricia had decided wanted to be the center post for our sleeping loft.

It was nearly dark, the bay pond-still and painted a yellow-orange by the setting sun, and we had supper waiting, but I measured the log against the loft, cut it to size with a chain saw, and Patricia and Greta and I heaved and twisted it into place. The log was sun- and sea-bleached almost white, and the sea had rounded and smoothed the stubs of its limbs into whorled knobs. It made a sturdy and beautiful old mast for the center of the cabin.

In five days I was going to have to fly to New York to sign a book contract that I hoped would let me quit worrying about our overextended budget in Nova Scotia. Omere would have to leave two days later, while I was still in New York, and I badly wanted to get the chimney installed and the window and door casings built—the two trickiest jobs left to do—before he left. I leaned on everyone again, and they responded generously. On the third day before I left we worked for thirteen hours— Omere on the casings, the rest of us, with Rob as foreman, on the siding—and everyone was in wonderful spirits. That night around the bonfire Greta invented a superhero called the Generalizer who leaps into any emergency, no matter how hopeless, with just the right banality to save the day (solving the country's health crisis, for example, with "A Stitch in Time Saves Nine"). We sat up for hours saving the world with Generalizer clichés.

The next morning Rob woke with a stomach virus and was sick for two days. Between trips to the outhouse he stayed in his tent, and Greta and Patricia brought him things he could eat. With Omere still working on the door and window casings, work on the siding slowed considerably without Rob's quick expertise at sizing and cutting the boards and his indefatigable, infectious energy.

Rob's parents are teen guidance counselors in the New Hampshire school system—radiant, high-energy people themselves, who believe in and lead a service-to-others life five days a week and are up at six on both days of their weekends to golf in the summers and ski in the winters, all day and always together. The McLeod family is a hearty stew of old-fashioned values: decency, commitment, loyalty, sacrificing for excellence, and working and playing with passion. In his senior year at Middlebury College, Rob won the national college championship in slalom skiing; he was president of his fraternity; a jock/scholar, the B.M.O.C. Since then in Jackson Hole he has worked construction and with kids, coaching young ski racers in the winter. Rob is an athletic virtuoso with good looks and great charm. In another family he might have been allowed to get by entirely on those qualities; in his, they hardly count. What people in and out of his family love Rob for are his quick, gentle wit, his people intelligence, his sensitivity to how and where he can help, his eagerness to put himself out, his unflinching loyalty. He has been my good, loved, and admired friend for years. We have hunted, fished, drunk, skied, and traveled together, sometimes just the two of us, and we had never had an argument or once come close to crossing swords until the second day of his tent-bound stomach flu.

"Gret—are you in there?" I shouted toward their tent. Wherever she was, she had been gone from the siding sweatshop for what I and her brothers thought was too long.

"Yes . . . Rob and I are talking."

"This is not the time for talking, Greta. The rest of us are working out here and I'd appreciate it if you'd join us." Hateful, I sounded—even to myself—and a hundred years old.

There was a long silence and no movement, then Rob said: "She's with me, Charles. She's going to stay here for a while."

This is a slippery slope for the father of a daughter to be on, and I have a temper. I could feel it coming up and actually opened my mouth to begin another war I couldn't win. Then I closed it again and walked back to the cabin.

"So, where is she?" asked Latham.

"Busy."

We badly needed a big trash bin, and that afternoon, partly to get me away from putting hammer dents in the cedar, Omere asked if I thought I could build one. I drew up a plan for a beauty, sort of half an A-frame. I gathered up materials and set up shop with a couple of sawhorses and a power saw on the deck of the blueberry shack. First I cut the floor of the bin out of plywood, then the two sloping sides. Instead of using one side as a pattern for the other, I tried to save some time by snapping the cuts with a chalk line, botched it, and wasted a sheet of plywood. It took me over an hour to measure and cut the four sides and the top and bottom for this overengineered box. Then I started screwing everything together with a power drill.

"What are you doing?" asked Rob. I was working just twenty feet from his tent and I realized he had been watching me all along through the mosquito netting.

"Building a trash bin."

After I screwed the four sides of the bin into the bottom, I put the top on it. It was too short.

Without my saying a word, Rob said, "I'll bet you took the inside measurements. You're an inch and a half off, aren't you?" From his tent he could tell this?

He came wobbling out, looking pale, and helped me recut the top and put the hinges on it. When we finished, I had been working on the bin for two and a half hours.

"It's good enough for East Tracadie," Rob said, and headed back for the tent.

"Thanks for the help," I said. "Hey, listen . . ." He turned around. "I'm sorry about earlier." He nodded. "Tell me the truth: How long would it have taken you to build this thing?"

"At least half an hour," he said and grinned. As usual, he was being kind.

The next morning I drove to Halifax and flew to New York, and no one but my dogs was sorry to see me go.

New York was astoundingly hot, with a sort of airless, doomsday heat, and as crowded and fever-pitched as it always is, but all those qualities were magnified by coming to them from the cool Canadian woods. I had a hard time sleeping in a bed, even the deluxe one I was borrowing from a bottled-water tycoon.

An old friend who is now a movie star and I were there to sign a contract for a series of books on fitness for kids. At the signing the president of the publishing company called the advance he was giving us "breaking the bank"; my movie star friend called working for that fee "charity." I didn't call it anything, but my half of the advance was just dandy by me. Over the past few years I had put in a good bit of work on kid fitness and the books were a chance to make that work pay off—for me, for a country full of out-of-shape children, and for a close friend and associate in that work who had died obscenely young. I knew I could make the books usable and valuable and that the movie star's name would get them into the hands of kids who needed them. That was all I needed to know to feel fine about taking the publisher's money, even though this was not what I had had in mind when I decided to start writing again. Other books could wait.

In the desperate heat and screech of New York, I could see as clearly as if it were billboarded in neon on Times Square how rare and precious a thing my family was doing in Nova Scotia, and it made me feel even finer to know that this money, this Big Apple wad of "congealed energy" as Joseph Campbell called it, wouldn't be wasted somewhere in a bank but shot straight into finishing off in style the building of a blue-roofed, cedar-sided family place by the sea. The truth is, knowing that made me feel like I was trading beads for Manhattan.

After the meeting at the publisher's office, I decided to walk the twenty-five blocks uptown to the apartment where I

was staying. On that walk I got caught in a thunderstorm that
clattered down Fifth Avenue whirling up dust and bits of paper,
darkening and then drenching the street in a rain of tracer
bullets that went on for half an hour. There were no taxis to be
had, of course, so I just started walking faster. All around me
people were doing the same, some with a practiced New York
stoicism on their faces; but others seemed excited by the rush
and immediacy of this heat-chasing downpour. I had the odd
urge to stop some of those people and tell them about our cabin
in Nova Scotia—the sudden open delight in their faces, maybe,
making me think they might want to hear about it. And block
by block I felt my own happiness growing—in this rain, this
hectic, improvised moment on Fifth Avenue, but also in our
cabin-building summer. Block by block that happiness swelled
in me as if it were being pumped in, until I thought I might be
lifted off the street by it. Wouldn't many of these hurrying
people love to be doing what we were doing? And wouldn't they
meet it by slowing down and treasuring every astonishing second of it? Would anyone in his right mind hurry through the
summer we were having just to get to the other side of it? I
started walking through puddles on purpose and grinning at
every person who looked at me. I decided to take my time
through the rain—there was nothing ahead of me that day that
could possibly be more fun anyway—and to enjoy every blessed
step.

It was early evening when I drove up the shale road to the
camp, three days after leaving it for New York. The sky had just
cleared from the northwest and it hung like a clean, pale-blue
vestment over the bay. The boys were working late on the cabin
and were as glad to see me as I was to see them. They had gotten

a lot of work done, both before and after Omere left: The door and window casings were finished, the "metalbestos" chimney was installed and connected to the interior stovepipe, the south and west walls were completely sided and the east wall well begun, and they had built a landing for the back door.

"Check this out, Dad," said Latham. He flipped the remote switch for the generator that we had wired underground into the pantry, and the cabin lit up. The electrician had come and installed outlets and sockets and we now had electric light.

"Jill and Mark weren't as impressed with it as we are," said Shelby. "They're under the impression everybody's got it."

Jill and Mark, friends from New York, were our first out-of-town visitors. They had driven up the day before in a big white car, said the boys, looking like tourists.

Rob said, "They pitched the blue tent, but it was a little windy and they thought they heard a coyote . . ."

"Mark called it a wolf," said Latham. "So they moved in here and slept on the worktable.

Shelby grinned. "I don't think they got much sleep. They thought it was cold and they couldn't figure out how to work the double sleeping bag. They were sort of quiet this morning, so Mom and Greta took them into Antigonish so they could see a shopping mall."

It was fun listening to this, even though the fun was at our city friends' expense. It was like seasoned troops talking about new recruits, veteran athletes about rookies, and I loved the hardship pride and brotherhood in their attitude.

When the rookies got back with Patricia and Greta, I cooked a supper on the deck and, after three nights in packed, overpriced New York restaurants, reveled in the richly simple pleasure of making a meal outdoors. I threw onto the grill some pork chops marinated in hot sauce and cumin, seared onions and red bell peppers in good olive oil over a wood fire, tossed in a few olives and jalapeños, and added rice. I made a salad, sliced a loaf of fresh bread, poured some wine into tin coffee cups, and we were there.

We ate by candlelight on the worktable inside the cabin, the window and door casings of the north wall opened to the stars, and played Billie Holliday on our battery-run boom box. For the first time in two weeks I felt my age again, or younger, and not at all hateful. A friend had invited me up to the Sevogle River in New Brunswick to fish salmon for the next three days, the July Fourth weekend, and told me I could bring two people. I had decided to go and to take Rob and Greta, since Greta would be leaving in a week to return to Wyoming. I told them this at dinner, and told Latham and Shelby they ought to take the weekend off and windsurf or take the boat out.

Jill is like a member of our family. She knows me. "What?" she said. "You're not in a hurry to get this cabin finished, Chuck?"

"Nope."

And I wasn't anymore; the impatience and tension I had felt since just after the storm now seemed blown out to sea.

Latham and Shelby did take the weekend off and enjoyed themselves with Patricia, Jill, and Mark. Greta, Rob, and I went salmon fishing in New Brunswick, and when we returned we all went back to work feeling fresh and relaxed. We slept later, took more time for lunch, and spent some afternoons water-skiing, windsurfing, kayaking, fishing, or hiking—and work on the cabin seemed to come along just as quickly as before. We painted and installed the beautiful, big, divided-light French doors that Patricia had found to place vertically all along the north wall and to use as horizontal windows on the east and west walls. That completely closed the cabin in, and some or all of us could have moved into it then, but we decided to wait until we were no longer working inside it. Omere, whom we greatly missed, had contended all summer that there were only two kinds of people in the world—those who eat their lobster bite by bite as they take it out of the shell, and those (like him) who wait until they have all the meat out before they eat any of it. We decided to take our pleasure in beginning to live in the cabin all at once, when it was fully ready to live in.

In the kitchen area we installed a propane oven and refrigerator, built some counters, and started on cabinets. In the bathroom we built a counter for the sink and put in a shower stall. Greta took the first hot shower in the cabin on the afternoon of July 9.

She was leaving for Wyoming two days later, so on the night of the tenth Greta threw herself a going-away party. In the month and two days since we had arrived, she had been our best ambassador to the community. While being a tireless camp chef and kitchen manager, she had found time the rest of us hadn't to visit in local homes and go to local parties, and she had made a lot of friends. Over forty of them came to her party.

It was a beautiful, warm evening. We set up borrowed folding chairs all around the blueberry shack and bonfire pit, smoked a pork roast, and made baked beans and pasta salad. Various guests brought chicken legs, meatballs, casseroles, bread, and cakes. Many of them also brought presents for Greta—flowers, a necklace, a sweatshirt, earrings—and gave them to her with a kiss. There was plenty of beer and rum and local moonshine. Nicole Andrews brought a case of tapes and deejayed for us, and when Greta and Rob started dancing on the deck after supper, it seemed just the thing to do, and before long the deck was crowded with dancing couples. Greta had invited lots of children, and they swarmed over the cleared area around the cabin playing football and baseball until the soft, late, midsummer dark fell. Then we made a bonfire and some of the guests and their children stayed and joined us around the fire for a while.

Greta, Shelby, and Latham played their guitars and sang, and children held on laps roasted marshmallows, and it was exactly, to the detail, as I had imagined this bonfire pit being used when I dug it and put up the seats a month ago. It was something more too for me, that scene—the quiet, close family joy of it, the warmth and heart's comfort and safety that was in it brought up a recollected reassurance from my childhood of Sunday dinners at my grandparents' house.

Greta came over and sat in my lap.

"We might even miss you," I told her.

"You will, because I'm the Glue of the Family. Do you know what the Generalizer would say?"

"What?"

" 'All's well that ends well.' I still think it's the most beautiful place I've ever seen. And now it's our place."

By midnight all the guests were gone, but we sat up a little later and let the fire go to embers. We tried out names for the cabin. And we were conscious of the beautiful, nearly finished little cedar building at the edge of the firelight, this "new organization" of our world and life, each member of our family, in a complex, independently proprietary way, as if it were a poem we were all writing together.

6

There is an ingenious graph that is sometimes used to demonstrate one of the fundamental curves along which modern nations and individuals define themselves. The vertical Y line of the graph stands for freedom, independence, options. The horizontal, or X, axis represents bonding, the shared values, laws, and other ties that have traditionally held societies and families together. Modern life requires of both individuals and societies a trade-off, a line pitched at some self-describing angle between the X and Y coordinates: The flatter that line, the more individual freedom and opportunity a person or a culture gives up; the steeper the line, the more bonds and ties are given up for options. Left to themselves, traditional cultures happily exist and define themselves along fairly flat lines. The twentieth century has universally raised the pitch of life within this graph, of course, and America in the 1980s chose to describe itself along an avalanche slope, off of which whole chunks of the society fell into bankruptcy and divorce, and less fortunate chunks into poverty, homelessness, and urban violence.

During the months that we were separated Patricia and I

both did a lot of fantasizing about our lives on the other side
of the misery we were caught in. My fantasies centered around
Patricia, and I did not figure in hers. But otherwise they were
very much alike: We both dreamed of a flatter life.

We had each in our own way been brought to bay and
treed by the three deadly creatures that Dante said stalk the
"dangerous forest" of our middle years, the very same beasts that
stalked the eighties: pride, desire, and fear. From my deserted
home in New Hampshire I had imagined the two of us in a
cabin or a trailer somewhere, in flannel shirts, reading by kero-
sene lamps with a soup on the stove, her work in one corner and
mine in another, and our kids coming over for supper. In New
York, haunted by an image of herself as a plant pulled by the
roots out of its pot and slowly dying, Patricia pictured some tall,
dark-haired man who knew how to be kind, a cozy country
home, and an adopted baby. Played out on options, and tired
of swimming against what John Updike calls that time's "tide
of endless wanting," we independently pined for nothing more
than a hearth and bonds—the constraints, the duties, the com-
mitments, the obligations, the chains even, of dedicated, inte-
grated love and work.

We were not the only ones in 1989 yearning for a recon-
nected life. With a national divorce rate of 50 percent, and the
American landscape littered with child abuse, welfare depen-
dency, crime, drug use, learning disabilities, and all the other
maimings of exploded families; with high-riding greed and ma-
terialism having turned consumerism into our most sacred and
celebrated national ritual; with millions of us having chased the
chimera of personal freedom into an existential black hole of
loneliness and longing; and with AIDS, overpopulation, world

hunger, and ecological disasters bearing down—those Four Horsemen of a New World Apocalypse, those killer embodiments of our own excesses and freedoms—more than a few other Americans wanted to rappel off the decade before things got any steeper and find a new way of living on the flats.

Some looked to the peaceful, family-centered hegemony of the fifties for a model of that way of living, and pictured what they had heard or remembered of that decade in Norman Rockwell images of Dad carving up the turkey of prosperous normalcy and passing it out to Mom and the kids. But Patricia and I didn't need any pop-culture images to illustrate for us the new life we wanted: We could look at that life in our own family albums. And as for an historical model of how life can be lived short on individual license but long on loving involvement with other people, delightedly sacrificing independence for ties, and lived that way religiously, as a daily joyous discipline—Patricia and I had Shook Hill to look to.

In the winter of 1920 my grandfather, Paschal Shook, and his brother Warner bought fifty acres of wild land on Shades Mountain, about five dirt-road miles south of Birmingham, Alabama. My grandfather was a prospering businessman in his late forties with a beautiful wife named Caroline and three young children, Mary Hansel, Paschal, Jr., and my mother, Margaret, who still remembers vividly her first visit to Shook Hill:

> One spring morning Mother and Daddy said, "Get into the car, we have something to show you." We skipped

breakfast, taking cold biscuit and bacon sandwiches, made the long ride down Highland Avenue past all the handsome homes of our friends, across Red Mountain, then down through the valley and up again on a small dirt road to Shades Mountain. There we came to a beautiful wilderness of forest, where Mother and Daddy and Uncle Warner and Aunt Anna had bought a large acreage and were going to build summer homes to get away from the heat of Birmingham.

My grandfather and his two brothers, Warner and Alfred, had come to coal- and iron-rich north Alabama from Nashville, Tennessee, in 1897, hoping to make careers for themselves in the mining business. Their father, Colonel Alfred Montgomery Shook, had made a fortune in the coal-and-iron business and kept a summer home himself in Tracy City, Tennessee, at which all of the Birmingham and Nashville Shooks would convene for three or four weeks each summer. The life there during those weeks was the template for Shook Hill.

My mother and her family, along with nurses, uncles, aunts, and cousins, would take the train from Birmingham to Chattanooga, then a smaller train up the mountain to Shook Station, which was right in front of Colonel Shook's big Victorian house. Tracy City was a country town with dirt streets and sidewalks of cedar shavings, pigs to chase, trees to climb, and picnics to be had at waterfalls and lakes. Cousin Peg Price had a dollhouse with a real wood stove, and there was a billy goat and cart for exploring. Eighteen or twenty family members would gather each evening for supper around a huge oak table and help themselves to garden vegetables, blackberry cobbler, and homemade ice cream. And after supper Peg Price and the older Hampton girls would sit on the porch, play the ukelele, and sing, "I Love You B-E-S-T Best of All the R-E-S-T Rest," and neighborhood boys would dart around the porch like swallows in the dusk. At bedtime the bunk rooms on the third floor were so full of giggling, whispering boys and girls that they were called "the streets of Cairo."

My grandfather and his brother Warner built their summer houses on Shades Mountain in 1921. Soon after that they added onto those houses, making them into year-round residences, and their younger brother, Alfred, joined them on Shades Mountain in the summers with his four children, bringing to ten the number of young cousins living on what their postman decided reasonably to rename Shook Hill.

It may be that no family life is without pain, but no pain that came from family life on Shook Hill is remembered by my mother. Life there for her and for the others who grew up there was, in fact, analgesic—a poultice for pain suffered elsewhere in the world—and throughout her youth and young womanhood it was as flawlessly sweet and Arcadian as the life pictured in nineteenth-century children's books or on the calendars that used to be given away by feed-and-grain stores.

There was a sleeping porch where the whole family would sleep on hot summer nights. There was a pasture with Jersey milk cows and saddle horses. There were vegetable and flower gardens, stables, and a barnyard full of chickens and turkeys. My mother and her brother and sister had a pet Plymouth Rock rooster named Tommy Alexander Shook and a pony named Bob. With their nurse, Kate, they hitched Bob up to a pony cart and went on blackberry hunts with a milk bottle of ice water and a box of soda crackers. They played with paper dolls and colored in painting books and built fairy meeting places out of rocks and moss. All summer long they played cowboys and Indians, hide-and-seek, and a game called "Mitt" in the woods between the two houses. Sometimes in the evenings they put on theatrical performances for the grown folks, using a sheet for a curtain and an unshaded standing lamp for a spotlight, and whenever their mother gave one of her formal dinner parties they would sit on the landing of the stairs and spy and giggle, and the small lamps with beaded pink shades and silver nut-and-mint baskets on the table would make them think of Hollywood.

Occasionally during the summer the kids on Shook Hill would be taken into town to a vaudeville show at the Lyric Theater, or to a movie starring Mary Pickford, Wallace Ford, Harold Lloyd, or Norma Talmadge. When she was older my mother and her cousin Alfred sometimes rode their horses for two hours to the livery stable in town, changed their clothes, went to lunch and a matinee, and then rode back home in the late afternoons. And during the school year she and her sister and brother were driven into town to school by their father in his old Dodge. But otherwise they rarely left Shook Hill and they rarely wanted to. Plenty of friends visited them there to spend a night or a weekend. When my mother and her sister were in their teens as many as twenty or thirty boys would come to call on Sunday afternoon to sit out on the big open pavilion, talk, and drink cold Jersey-cow buttermilk.

Shook Hill was always a welcoming, social place—meeting visitors with good country food and lively company, with comfortable guest rooms, fresh flower arrangements throughout the house in the summer, and big, open fires in the winter. My grandmother was a great party-giver, a skilled collector of books and antiques, and an ardent traveler; my grandfather was a popular business and civic leader who was admired throughout northern Alabama. The two of them had many friends and interests and they brought those friends and interests home with them. But they saved the best of themselves and their home for themselves and their children, their brothers and sisters and parents and aunts and uncles and cousins—and that made Shook Hill also, profoundly, a family place. My grandfather went to his office every day of the week until he was ninety-two, but he rode horseback for an hour with my mother each morning before he left for work, and he never missed six o'clock supper with his family. When one of his children was away from Shook Hill he wrote that child a letter a day. And nothing in life gave that magisterial man as much pleasure as playing on the floor with grandbabies.

His wife, "Carrie," was his heart—and the heart of Shook Hill. As lovely, clear, and finely turned as one of the pieces of crystal she collected, she seemed to spill off light as she whistled and sang through the house at homemaking. She had exquisite tastes, a jaunty pride, and a fiercely active and individuated love for every member of her family. Carrie harmonized people. Just her presence made discord or unpleasantness seem impossible, and my mother says she never knew her to say even a slightly mean or ugly word or express an unlovely thought.

Sunday dinner was usually an extended family meal at her house, with often as many as fifteen people around the formal dining table sharing homegrown chickens and vegetables, homemade butter, beaten biscuits, and peach ice cream. Carrie would be at one end of the table and Paschal at the other, and between them the soul-delighting reassurance of Shook Hill would hang in the air like the tone from a struck crystal water glass: the shared knowledge that the people at this table were not only each other's family but each other's closest friends, each other's greatest joy, each other's refuge—and that they would continue to be all of that to each other for as long as they lived.

Over the years other members of the family built houses on Shook Hill. At one point in the sixties there were seven Shook-related families living there, and the big holiday parties at my grandparents' house might have at them as many as forty family members representing four generations. During this time Shook Hill was often referred to as a "family compound," but it was something at the same time simpler and more complicated than that. People who were not family members, a few, bought land and built houses there beginning in the 1930s. My grandfather and his brother were never interested in keeping nonfamily members off of Shook Hill but in creating a life there that would keep family members on it. And they did that, they and their wives, by making Shook Hill come to be the center of their children's spiritual geography—the place from which the world felt safest and best made sense. Not all of those children, nor all of their children, have had completely happy lives; Shook Hill didn't give a lifetime warranty on happiness. But it did give the people who lived there a bedrock consciousness of the sacredly interlocking joys and responsibilities of family life and a hearth—built around a constant fire of love and commitment—at which they could warm themselves, happy or not, all their lives.

What in 1920 was a dirt road leading down from Shades Mountain into the city of Birmingham is now a hazardous four-lane highway. There are still Shooks on Shook Hill, but a big part of the property was sold in the 1980s and developed into a pretentious clutch of enormous houses called Shook Hill Estates. Shook Hill as a way of living doesn't exist anymore, except as starter coals carried by the people who sat around its hearth.

Hearth is heat, heart, and earth combined—a place, an "earth," of the heart that provides heat against the cold of the world. In our earliest history the hearth was a revetment against night and the creatures that prowled the night—and much more. It was the original "family circle" around a fire where people warmed themselves and ate, gave birth, told stories, made and repaired clothes and tools—the place where life originated and was sustained and where the skills and values of living were passed along from elders to children. The hearth should be, profoundly, a family place, but also a social place—a place of common meals, of the communion of family and friends, and the gathering of community. It should keep at bay what is cold and dangerous and invite in whatever loves the light and heat it surrounds, creating around itself growing rings of connections, from nuclear to extended family, to something like a tribe.

The writer and philosopher Sam Keen has described the fully socialized hearth as

> a place of gathering, a center where friends and family talk about what is important; feast, laugh and work together; celebrate the rites of passage that punctuate their days; witness and pledge common troth with bride and groom;

christen and initiate children; rejoice together in good fortune, new jobs, and successful undertakings; give aid, advice and consent in handling delinquent children, alcoholic wives, and lovers and friends with cancer; tend senile parents; and care for strangers who come into their midst.

Sam Keen believes that a return to the hearth is our salvation as individuals—and might yet be the salvation of the earth:

> The great calling of our time that is worthy of men and women is to hold each other within our hearts, and to conspire to create a hearth within the earth household.
>
> These three live or die together: The Heart. The Hearth. The Earth.

The ancient Greeks revered the hearth as a place of sacrifice, celebration, and peace. In Greek mythology Zeus's sister Hestia was goddess of the hearth, and every meal began and ended with an offering to her. She was also the first of the deities to be invoked in Greek sacrifices and the only one who did not like to fight.

Every city in ancient Greece had a public hearth that was sacred to Hestia, and the fire in that hearth was never allowed to go out. Whenever a new city was to be founded, the founders would carry with them coals from the hearth of the mother city with which to begin the fire on the new city's hearth. In that way—with the coals from an old hearth kindling the flame on a new one—were the traditions and teachings of Hestia passed along.

*   *   *

When Patricia and I came back together in the summer of 1989 we both knew exactly what kind of life we did not want any more—and something of what we did want. More important, both of us were free of some old trappings and able for the first time in years to make a new start. Patricia knew finally that she did not want to live or work ever again in either New York or the root cellar of her subconscious, and she had given up forever dredging her unhappy childhood for images.

And I had stopped caring about being tough. For a while I had wanted to be a tough guy, and then for a while I was one and could put myself through any physical pain or test without making a sound and come out swinging. I studied and learned all the male action that goes with putting a premium on toughness—all those moves that are as stylized as the moves in Kabuki drama, until I could make them backward in my sleep— and I adopted the thinking that lets you make them instinctively. Then life had the good grace to teach me exactly where I am not tough and never will be and that toughness and half a buck will buy you a cup of coffee. And that was that: It felt like I had just opened a door, walked through it, and closed it again, and on that new side of the door at least half of what had been important to me for most of my life didn't matter anymore.

After we bought the land in Nova Scotia, the property itself revealed to Patricia and me over a period of months more and more of what we wanted from a new life, and by the late fall a composite had emerged: We wanted a chance to reclaim real intimacy with each other and our children; we wanted calm, appropriate boldness, simplicity, connections, selective work and play, and a new and vital hearth. We still had coals from Shook Hill and other places to carry to that hearth. But what should it look like? How exactly should we build it?

Over the winter Patricia found an idiosyncratic, lovable book, published in 1945, called *Your Cabin in the Woods* by Conrad E. Meinecke, a man who built thirty-two cabins and fireplaces for himself in the woods throughout the Rockies and Canada. Meinecke truly loved cabins. He saw them as outposts of new hope, each one snugly housing its own specific dream. And he loved to work outward from these cabins toward whatever interlocking possibilities the site provided, discovering those possibilities one by one and integrating them into a long-term vision for the place.

Meinecke was no woodsy reductionist. In creating his various hearths he was not after, as Thoreau was, "a stern and more than Spartan simplicity of life," but rather a rustic richness. Thoreau went to the Massachusetts woods to be alone and to whittle as spare a creature life as possible. He wanted "to drive life into a corner, and reduce it to its lowest terms," then stalk away to write in his journal or read his Homer. The hearth he kept at Walden was a narrow one, around an economical fire, with room at it for only one and with a sign posted nearby reading: SIMPLIFY, SIMPLIFY. INSTEAD OF THREE MEALS A DAY, EAT BUT ONE. NO SAUCE ON THE PASTA.

Meinecke, on the other hand, was a builder of voluptuous hearths, to which he welcomed anyone of kindred spirit to watch the stars and knife into one of his expertly grilled steaks. "Listen to the grease drip into the hot coals," he invites you. "Watch it jump into the flames. Good! Let it burn. Let the

flames play around the steaks for about three minutes wildly!"
And then,

> The meal over with, you will soon start singing folk
> songs, chatting, singing again. Someone brings a guitar or
> banjo. Soon there are blinking stars. Again a lovely night.
> In season we find lovely, inspiring nights in any part of
> this global world. Let's use them. Call in your family, your
> guests, your friends, for a supper about your outdoor
> garden fireplace.

Meinecke believed that cabin life, with its isolation, its
shared chores and plain needs, is the best possible format for
communion with other people; and he believed that in the
course of that life our true concerns, the things that really matter
to us, will emerge clearly as such, making fellowship that much
more meaningful. He also believed that living in the woods
should be fun rather than stoical, playful as well as practical, and
more about maximizing than minimizing. So, in addition to
nuts-and-bolts information on picking a site, drainage and grad-
ing, and cabin construction, *Your Cabin in the Woods* tells you how
to build fancy gates, wrought-iron andirons and pot holders,
rustic furniture, and a swing for the garden. It shows you how
to make a walkway of stepping stones, a meat-basting spoon,
and a "four o'clock tidbit" of cinnamon-sugar toast for your
guests. And it waxes at length on friendliness, the beauty of
lantern light and storms, landscaping, and being a good neighbor to birds. Good cabin living, Meinecke suggests, like good
living anywhere, is largely in the details.

What Patricia and I found most wonderful about the

book was the diagram shown below called "Legend of Family Campground." Here was an actual plan, bristling with detail, for elaborating outward from a single tent or cabin to a simple but complete community of fellowship and fun, a small, vivid,

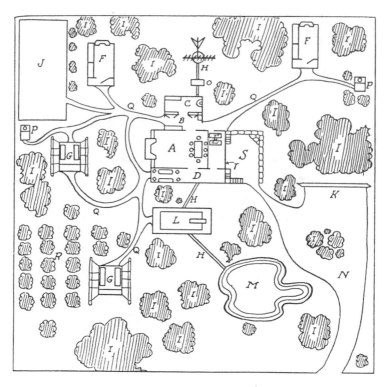

LEGEND OF FAMILY CAMP GROUNDS

A . Main Living Room
B . Kitchen
C . Wash and Storeroom
D . Veranda
E . "Master Bedroom" on Porch
F . Guest Cabin
G . Guest Tent
H . Windmill and Water System
I . Shade Trees
J . Tennis Court or Vegetable Plot

K . Parking Lot
L . Swimming Pool   9 by 15 feet
M . Lily Pond
N . Driveway
O . Hot Water Heater
P . "Johnnie"
Q . Trails
R . Fruit Trees
S . Sunken Garden - Outdoor Fireplace
T . Shower under veranda

particular vision of Eden, one it took Meinecke over twenty years to realize, of happy family and friends passing each other in the woods over well-designed paths on their way to work and play. It is the blueprint of a master hearth-builder's ultimate hearth, built on the flat, and Patricia and I knew the instant we saw it that it was very like what we wanted for ourselves.

Patricia gave me *Your Cabin in the Woods* for Christmas and we pored over it for months, studying the diagrams and floor plans for ways and means. By the time we left for Nova Scotia we had in mind the basic progressions of our own long-term vision—each image distinct, sequential, and riper than the one before, like a series of time-elapsed nature photos of the opening of a flower—from tent camp to cabin, to a big Adirondack-style common building with a number of cabins surrounding it full of family and close friends, to wind and solar power, a big vegetable and flower garden ringed by tall Carolina poplars, a pond, a road down to a boat house on Linwood Harbor, a writing shack, a studio for Patricia . . . And illuminating that vision for us, like a cast of noon light, was the abiding reassurance of Shook Hill.

As it turned out, our images of the first summer in Nova Scotia were accurate, but they were incomplete. There was nothing in them of an agonizing loss.

7

My son the Judge and I are
going to fly a kite. It is midmorning, July 21, the day before he
leaves Nova Scotia to drive to Alabama to take a job in his
cousin's music studio for the rest of the summer. After that he
plans to move to Jackson Hole, Wyoming, to join his brother
and sister in working out there. For twenty-two years his home
has been with Patricia and me. Wherever we were, Shelby was.
Tomorrow he launches into his own life, as the other two have
already done, and from then on my time with him will be
coincidental, a few days here or there, as it already is with his
brother and sister. This day is a hinge for both of us; the last
day of a particular angle we have had to each other for twenty-
two years and we want to spend part of that day together before
it burns a hole in our pockets.

"Every day is a god, each day is a god, and holiness holds
forth in time," is how Annie Dillard begins her ravishing little
book of life worship called *Holy the Firm*. Each day is a god
indeed up here, and we have met them in all stripes. This day's
god is impulsive and playful, a handsome tease. Fat white clouds
scurry across the sun in front of him like spooked broiler hens,

and his mischief has kicked up a brisk wind off the bay. It is our kind of day, and Shelby and I take the dogs and the kite, leave Latham and Rob to finish building the deck off the front of the cabin, and go off to have some sport with this bad boy god.

Last week John Mattie came up with his tractor and a bush hog and cut a network of trails out on the cape. Shelby and I follow one of these, and Fields and Arthur run through the brush nosing out creatures. This matted, bristling brush has an almost urban density and variety of life in it. Sparrows, meadowlarks, and canaries flit through it; rabbits, chipmunks, foxes, porcupines, and deer make homes in it, and coyotes prowl it at night. Crisscrossed with animal paths, it is nearly a full square mile of overlapping scent trails, and our two bird dogs go into a happy frenzy in it chasing down smells.

Arthur enthusiastically belongs to one of the pointing breeds, which means that he announces having smelled out something he thinks you should be interested in by stopping dead still and pointing at it with his nose, head, body, and tail all in an emphatic line, a sort of horizontal exclamation mark that says to you, "There it is—go shoot it!" Normally a phlegmatic and discriminating soul, Arthur wouldn't dream of bothering to point anything but a game bird while hunting, but here in this odorous brush he runs around flash-pointing songbirds and rabbits like a puppy—locking up for a few seconds, then loping off in his chesty, rocking horse gait after a new scent and looking back at me once in a while like a butler caught on a tear.

Fields is a retriever, trained to flush birds up within range of a gun and then to bring back to you in his mouth whatever you shoot. When he is on a scent, his big golden tail goes around in a circle and his face gleams and grins with pleasure.

More fleet and graceful than Arthur, Fields seems younger too, though they are both five. He is jaunty where Arthur is deliberate, effusive where Arthur is discreet. When Arthur is actually hunting, he does so with manic single-mindedness; through cut paws, snow, exhaustion, or all-day rain, Arthur's amber eye is always on the ball. Fields loves his hunting too, but only when it is fun. Galloping around now in the bush, his tail windmilling, he has none of Arthur's slightly embarrassed air over this bogus hunting—this is the part of hunting he most enjoys anyway, running around joyfully and decoratively following his nose, and the glances he throws back to Shelby and me are purely delighted.

Shelby and I too are delighted to be out following our noses on this show-off morning. Sea gulls and crows glide and yawp over the end of the cape. A marsh hawk cruises the brush looking for brunch, and the young bald eagle we have come to know traces languid circles over our heads. To the ancient Greeks all of nature was display, showcasing the character and moods of the gods in the shapes of clouds, in storms, in peacocks strutting and the dances of herons. The entire natural world was like a show of fireworks where one display activates the next, where the visual energies of a moment that can be caught and held—that moment's sacred character—are answered by more defining visual energies, and those by more. A wind blows, a tree bends, a leaf falls . . . and so does the world become an unfurling scroll of revelation, of holiness holding forth in time.

Shelby and I get into our day's act at the end of the cape by popping into the air a huge hexagonal orange and yellow kite with red and blue streamers flying from its tail. It soars off into the crisp sky in a series of hungry swoops, ripping nylon cord off the big two-handled reel. Judge holds the handles lightly and lets the spool of the reel spin between his hands and in no time the kite is a hundred yards above us to the south—a plunging bright shield in the sky, now on display with eagle and hawk, crows and gulls, sea and shore, a father and son, and two dogs flushing the brush.

Shelby has always loved kites, as I have, and flying them together has been a shared pleasure of ours for years. I lay in the grass at the lip of the cliff and watch him—and think of him catching his own wind and soaring away tomorrow. I think: Patricia and I have twenty-two years of string to hold him by, and I make a quick prayer to the various emanations of this day that there is no place in that string so frayed that it will break when we try to reel him back in to this place.

"I'm sorry we didn't fish more this summer," I say. "I'm sorry we didn't get into the bass with Nick."

Shelby is watching the kite. His face is happy and calm. I think of how comfortable he is with himself, with both his hard and soft places, and how free of affectation he is, and how happy and calm and sound he is with his life. And I feel a stab of mingled love and fear for him, as I have done thousands of times since he was born.

He says, "I'm not sorry. We did what we came up here to do. We can fish next summer."

"I worried too much. I could've made things more fun."

Shelby begins to walk the kite down the bluff toward Linwood Harbor. Fields and Arthur have come in, and Fields is jumping up on Shelby, trying to take the kite reel in his mouth. My son lifts the reel over his head and gentles the kite down the bluff against the strong wind. Watching him—too close to the edge of the sheer sixty-foot cliff and not looking where he's going—the gremlin fear that lives in the deep center of my life, the fear of some freak, string-snapping gust that would break one of my children off from me for good, jumps into my chest and sits there staring. I stand up and follow Shelby. I want to tell him, "Watch where you're going," but I don't. "I guess I just worried too much," I say again.

As I walk toward him, trying not to hurry, the gremlin spits out an image, one of those burned-in-the-brain images that after a while are all we have left of our children's childhoods. In this one Shelby is four years old and he has blood all over his face. When he was little he had occasional nosebleeds. One day while we were driving someplace he stood up in the back of the car and leaned over the front seat between me and Patricia. "I'm in trouble," he announced, and blood started running from his nose and covered his lower face and neck. I whipped the car to a stop on the side of the road and Patricia and I pulled the Judge into the front seat and put his head down in my lap. He looked up at me, blinking calmly and not crying, the blood still running, and I sat there praying it would stop and wishing I could somehow push it back up into his head.

"It was a wonderful summer, Dad," he says now. "You didn't mess anything up. You made it happen, and what happened was great."

I pull his tall, skinny self to me, away from the cliff, and hug him hard, and the gremlin goes back into hiding.

We fly the kite, taking turns with it, and walk the bluff toward Linwood Harbor. Tired now and panting, Arthur walks with us and Fields runs out ahead. Just as we start downhill into the cup of land at the mouth of the harbor, Fields stops at the cliff's edge and begins barking down at the beach, which here is some forty feet below him. Shelby and I catch up to him and look down. On the stones and sand at the base of the cliff, lapped by an incoming tide, is a big, dead, and bloated fish.

"Is it a dolphin?" says Shelby.

"I don't know. Let's go find out." I hand Shelby the kite reel and we jog down the lowering bluff to a place where we can scramble to the beach. My hips are hurting from the walking. I struggle to keep up with Shelby, feel a dank little intimation of mortality, and try not to show that I am struggling. Fields has stayed where he was and is still barking at the fish. Arthur has stopped beside him and is also looking over the cliff. I shout to both of them as Shelby and I start down what is now a gradual slope to the beach and Arthur trots along the cliff toward us, but Fields paws a couple of times at the edge and then jumps directly down the slope.

"Oh my God," says Shelby. Though it does look like a suicide and my breath catches in my throat, I have seen Fields do too many amazing, death-teasing dances of balance and agility on steep slopes while rock and mountain climbing with me—I know Fields is immortal. He is in the air for a second, then he hits the nearly vertical red-clay slope with his forelegs braced stiff and his back legs folded under him. He slides that way for about twenty feet before he tumbles, rolling over to his left and head over heels, but he comes up sliding again, facing uphill now and clawing at the clay, and then just before he crashes into the rocks at the bottom he lets go his grip on the slope, somehow throws himself upright in mid-air—and lands lightly on all four feet.

Fields shakes himself and trots over to lap some seawater. Arthur, who has watched all this from the bluff, yawns, lies down, and puts his head on his paws. Shelby and I run to the beach.

The fish is a young bluefin tuna of maybe a hundred pounds. A deep chunk has been taken out of its back by a boat's propeller or a shark, and it has been dead for a couple of days. Fields stalks around it gravely. Some animals appear to share some of our elaborate emotions about death. Sea mammals, elephants, and otters evidently mourn their dead, as do some dogs. Fields is always serious and attentive around death, even the deaths of the ducks we hunt together, as though he is in on the secret that the God who made this universe wasn't joking. I bury my hands into the spun gold hair on his back and rub the ribs of this dog that means the world to me, and Shelby hands me the kite reel and sits down to examine him for cuts or bruises. Fields licks Judge's face. The sun comes out from behind a cloud and whacks us there on the beach. The tide is coming in before the wind and hissing in the pebbles of shale, our kite prances over the bluff, and this moment seems to hang for hours on display.

The amazing thing is not that we die in the passage of time, but that we are able to grasp and hold with our minds and senses for certain moments during that passage the stone sureness that we are alive. Watching my son who is leaving and my duck dog who is not, I think: God is like a duck hunter, concealed in the ultimate blind of the universe, and he calls us in to life as well as death.

"Give us time," prayed the great Trappist monk Thomas Merton.

And then I reel in the kite, learning again as if I had never known that the trick to bringing it home is all in the feel for when to give slack and when to take it in.

When Shelby and I got back to the cabin with the dogs, Latham and Rob had finished the deck, Patricia had made a tuna salad for lunch, and the honey wagon was back to pump the indoor outhouse again.

Omere's ingenious idea for our toilet system had not worked. Every time it rained the underground plywood box filled with water that sat there for days breathing odors into the cabin before being absorbed by the red-clay soil. This was the third time we had had to have the thing pumped out—at a price—and there are few more depressing ways to spend your money. We knew we would have to put in a septic system, but we also knew that that major expense would have to wait for next summer, so for the time being we were left with a honey-wagon operator who prayed for rain.

The indoor outhouse notwithstanding, our cabin in the woods was becoming more and more livable. The kitchen and bathroom were now fully plumbed and functional. We had installed wall-hung propane lamps for light when we didn't want to run the generator and had finished off most of the cabin's interior in sweet-smelling cedar. We had built into the southwest corner of the cabin a high, queen-size bed from which you could watch the sun rise out of Linwood Harbor and set over Cape George and see the fishing boats going out to work in the early morning. We had built bookshelves, a closet, an eight-foot dining table with driftwood legs, pantry shelves, an elegant ladder to the sleeping loft, and a driftwood coffee table. And we had finished installing the kitchen cabinets, counters, and drawers.

We had been helped in some of this labor recently by our friends Hayes and Patricia Noel, who had flown out from San Francisco for a five-day visit. They arrived on July 14, our second pair of out-of-town visitors, and Patricia and I and the boys feasted on their presence. Latham, Shelby, and Rob were sleeping in the loft by then, but Patricia and I were still occupying our tent, still waiting until every morsel of meat was out of the lobster before we ate. The Noels stayed in the other big, green PineTree Lodge tent and loved it. We took them to the Highland Games in Antigonish to watch beefy Scotsmen in kilts tossing the caber and hammer to bagpipe music. We drove up to Baddeck to the Alexander Graham Bell Museum, went kayaking and water-skiing and mackerel fishing. We took long evening walks on the beach with these old friends and they worked on the cabin in the mornings with us. We cooked up lobsters and Missouri chicken and grilled salmon at night, sang and told stories around the bonfire, then played darts and drank cognac in the cabin to propane light until after midnight. It was a fine, full five days, charged with Hayes's and Patricia's joy in our place and our venture, and when they flew back west they left us with a refreshed vision of what we were doing and new energy for doing it.

The evening after the honey-wagon man had come and gone, Shelby's last evening in Nova Scotia, we moved some chairs, the picnic table, and the grill out onto our broad new deck and cooked an early supper there. Around eight the kite-flying wind that had been tearing around all day went down, the sea went flat, and the boys went inside the cabin for a game of darts. Patricia and I stayed out on the deck, swatting mosquitoes now and then, to watch the sunset do a stirring riff with only two colors, pink and baby blue. A single sailboat was becalmed off of Blue Rock Cape, tiny in the vast sweep of the bay, and Patricia said: "Big landscapes are restful, aren't they? I mean, all those little, tiny vistas in New England make you think you can have them for lunch. They make you want to go out and build fences and take the rocks out of fields. But these really big views—they're too big to do anything with, and that's very relaxing."

The sunset played on imaginatively over Patricia's big view, reminding us of Joan Baez's "Dee Da" song that goes both simply and ornately up and down a scale, from lascivious to ecclesiastical with just two sounds, and Patricia and I sat on the deck watching the day's last display—and then continued to sit well into the quiet dark.

After Shelby left for Alabama we went into what Rob called low gear, moving slowly but with good traction, working on the cabin until lunch and taking the afternoons off to do whatever we pleased. We built bench seats on the deck and shelves for the bathroom. We painted the cabin's plywood floor a smoky blue, put up window boxes for flowers, planted pots with herbs, and tilled a big vegetable garden for the following summer. Patricia and I went to a secondhand store and bought two old Brazilian cow skins for rugs, a couple of wicker rocking chairs, and two big wooden armchairs to put in front of the wood stove. We hung a curtain in the shower, bought dish towels and cheap wine glasses, and built a wood box.

Then we looked up one day, the last day of July it was, and

realized we were finished. Everything we had wanted to do was
done, a little over six weeks after it was begun. That afternoon
I went out to the shed and hung up my tool belt on a nail, where
it would stay until we left Nova Scotia some three weeks later.
To be honest, I was not at all sorry to hang it there. Six weeks
of daily intimacy with the various devices in that belt had not
much improved my skill with any of them, though I did feel I
had come to know them a bit, in an imperfect way. Carpentry
tools are refreshingly specific things and using them appropri-
ately and well is the best way to know them. But failing that, it
is hard to resist a metaphorical approach: There are the brutes,
the crowbar and the huge maul we used to knock the corner
posts of the house into line; there is the high-strung, unforgiving
little wood chisel, that is best kept muzzled in a leather sheath
until it, and only it, is called for; and there is the level   who
would not like to have one of these adapted to lay along a
business deal, a friendship, or a marriage to see where the bubble
comes up between the lines?

All the meat was now out of the shell, and on the first of
August Patricia and I moved into the cabin. I went into Antigonish and bought four bottles of wine and Patricia, Latham,
and Rob went down to the beach at low tide and gathered a
bucketful of clams and mussels. For supper we had the shellfish
over fresh pasta and a tomato-and-goat-cheese salad with basil
from our pots on the deck, and we drank all four bottles of
wine. Later, the boys went into town to a movie and Patricia and
I went to bed.

When I turned off the propane lamp over our bed, the
glamorous, skim-milk light from a full moon poured through
the French-door windows on the cabin's east wall and covered

the interior of the cabin. Patricia and I lay in our high bed and looked at the center post, the wood stove and chimney, the ladder to the loft, the dining table and kitchen—all of it lacquered with the blue-white moonlight. We could see a starry sky through the west window and the dark sea through the eight French doors facing north. After a half hour or so our resident coyotes began their nightly chorus of yips and howls. Patricia and I lay in the bed holding each other, listening to them—at home, the two of us together, in a place illuminated like a dream. And the summer seemed won to me then for the first time. There seemed to be no lurking danger and urgency left in that soft night beyond the cabin.

The cabin had gone up quickly, as planned, and only somewhat over budget. (All labor and materials, the road, the well, site preparation, and all the gear I had bought and brought up for the project came to less than what you might pay for a Mercedes.) But neither planning nor the day-to-day experience of building the cabin had prepared us for the delight we felt with the finished product once we moved into it. We wandered around inside and outside the little building, admiring how the sun gave the cedar a honey-colored glow and how the roof picked up the exact color of the bay at certain times. Inside during the day the cabin was full of light and glimpses of sea, and at night, as we read, threw darts, or played board games, the living area seemed to hum with the soft propane light and the reassuring smell of cedar.

My mother, my sister Hansell and two of her sons, and an old friend named John Gunn came up together from Alabama for a visit in the first week of August. Disliking our bathroom situation, my mother and sister stayed in a hotel in Antigonish; John and my nephews took over the tents. Hansell liked the area so much that before she left she bought a twenty-acre piece of land contiguous to ours in Linwood Harbor.

Her husband is dead, as is my father—two men, as Hansell and my mother observed at different times, who would have loved this piece of sea-wrapped land—and both women enjoyed thinking of their husbands there with us, filling their two big gaps in the family circle, around a new family hearth.

My mother said that something about the place reminded her of Shook Hill. Joking, I think, but maybe half serious, she asked me if I would build her a little house in a grove of spruces overlooking Tracadie Harbor. She sat in Tom and Mary Mattie's living room seeing Nova Scotian fiddling and clog dancing for the first time on television with a delighted grin of surprise on her beautiful eighty-two-year-old face. And she lay on our bed in the cabin one rainy afternoon and wrote out for her brother back in Alabama a list of sixteen things she liked about this place. "Kind, hard-working, family people for neighbors," was first on the list; "Lots of time to read" was number four. Just before she left she looked me in the eyes and said, exactly, "You have created a little paradise up here, Charles . . . Don't screw it up."

Despite that warning, Patricia and I no longer really believed that this adventure of ours could be screwed up until the following week, when our last visitors of the summer, Stanley and Linda, arrived. Stanley and Linda are two of our most treasured friends. We have known him for over twenty years and her for the three years they have been married. Stanley is a film director, and he and I once worked on a movie together. The four of us have traveled together. Patricia and I have stayed in their Los Angeles home, and they have stayed with us in New Hampshire. The autumn before, when I had been trying to scrape up the money to buy the seventy additional acres on Linwood Harbor, Stanley had offered to buy half of it, site unseen. He had never been to Nova Scotia and he thought it unlikely that he and Linda would ever want to build a house there. Neither of them much liked the outdoors, and their idea of roughing it was having to drink vin ordinaire with dinner. Stanley would buy half the harbor property as an investment, he said, but Patricia and I knew he was really doing it to help us out. Fine, Patricia and I said to each other at the time: That land *was* a good investment, and someday if they wanted us to buy them out, Stanley and Linda could make a nice profit on it. In the meantime, it would be like having the land all to ourselves, since they would probably never use it. And if they wanted to come up once in a while for a visit, great.

Stanley is a very good director who doesn't always get along well with other human beings, particularly the ones he works with. He comes from Hollywood aristocracy—a powerful family of directors, producers, and studio heads. Stanley was the only son in one branch of this family, and growing up he learned how to shout a lot. On the set he can, and often does, terrorize crew members and actors by stomping around, shouting, and making fierce. But anyone who knows Stanley well pays no attention to these frequent professional rages, knowing them to be part of a persona that Stanley has created to make a living for him and behind which he has managed to stay fully human in a business that frequently turns people into crocodiles. The rages have nothing to do with the real Stanley, who is an unmitigated sweetheart, generous and kind to a fault. But the real Stanley rarely shows up with many people—and some of those people would insist that Stanley has become, as Socrates advised us all to do, what he wishes to seem.

Stanley and Linda arrived at the cabin around three o'clock in the afternoon of a hot, perfectly beautiful day. They had flown early from Los Angeles to Halifax, then driven the two and a half hours to East Tracadie, and they were tired. Stanley, moreover, was acutely annoyed because his cellular phone had stopped working some two miles from the cabin in the middle of a conversation with a movie actor whom he referred to as "the Runt." When Patricia and I walked out to greet them, he was standing beside his rented Lincoln Town Car, dressed in an Hawaiian shirt and poking furiously at the little phone. We hugged Linda.

"He's being awful," she groaned. "Let's just go inside and leave him out here for the wolves to eat." She looked around. "Do we have wolves?"

"What we don't have is cellular service," shouted Stanley. He folded up the phone and put it in his shirt pocket. "The Runt is going to be some pissed. He'll think I hung up on him, which I was about to do anyway. Heh, heh, heh." He pulled Patricia into a bear hug. "So, howaya?"

"Wonderful," said Patricia. "Why do you call him 'the Runt'? I thought he was a big guy."

"Magic'a Hollywood," said Stanley. "Hey Linda!" he shouted at the back of his wife, who was carrying a Gucci bag toward the cabin. "Tricia says she's wonderful and she's livin' with this jerk." Then he looked at me for the first time and grinned. "Hey Challie, why do JAPs close their eyes while they're doing it?"

"I don't know."

"So they can pretend they're shopping." He opened his big, hairy arms. "Give us a hug, Jerk."

After we got Stanley and Linda moved into the cabin, Linda decided they should move out again—to a motel. "It's nice," she said. "It's lovely here, but we don't want to get on anybody's nerves. Stanley gets on everybody's nerves. Even in six-bedroom houses he gets on everybody's nerves."

We called a motel in town and reserved them a room. Then we asked them if they wanted to take a walk over the property.

"Are there bugs?" asked Linda.

"A few mosquitoes," Patricia said, "but not until later."

Stanley said, "I want to see the property we have together. It's probably in a swamp, Linda! Challie—this land where we are now, is this ours together?"

"No. That's down on the harbor."

"You see, Linda—all the high, *nice* land, the land with a view, that's theirs by themselves. We're down in a mine shaft someplace." He put his arm over Patricia's shoulder. "Whatdya get when you cross a JAP and a hooker?" he asked her.

"What, Stanley?"

"Someone who sucks credit cards."

We walked them down to the cape, with Stanley talking nonstop about the movie he was hoping to make with the Runt, and then down the bluff to Linwood Harbor, which was silver with late afternoon light. I showed Stanley and Linda the boundaries of the land we owned jointly, and then we bush-whacked through thick brush and a dense stand of spruces to a little clearing, an old house site near the center of the property. It was a beautiful spot, surrounded by old apple trees and tall, mature spruces with a stunning view of the sea, but it was not easy to get to. Stanley and Linda were puffing and scratched when we finally made the clearing.

"Here we are," I told them.

"Where? Where's where we are? Nowhere, that's where," said Stanley. "Linda, I told you we'd be at the bottom of a mine shaft. And what's with this heat? I thought Canada was cool. Weather's gonna be better tomorrow, though, right? Rain, probably."

"Shut up, Stanley, and look at the view," said Linda. And he actually looked for a few seconds without saying a word.

"The view's nice," he acknowledged finally, snapping out of what passes for reverie with Stanley. "You could put a house here. How far is it to the beach?"

"Not far," I told him. "Next summer I want to put a road from our cabin down to the beach. It would go right by here."

"Now *waaait* a minute, Challie. How do I know I'm going to want a road going through here? What if this is where Linda and I decide to build and you've put a road through the middle of it, with tourists driving by, and . . ."

"Stanley," said Patricia.

"A private road, Stanley, like a driveway," I said.

Stanley held up a wise, advising hand and wagged it near his forehead. "It starts *out* a private road, maybe . . ."

"Can we talk about all this over a glass of wine?" asked Linda. "I'm getting bitten by something."

"These mosquitoes you got here are cousins to the ones in

Grand Isle, Louisiana," said Stanley. "I did a picture down there and those mosquitoes are just like the ones you *don't have here until later.* They work in teams—half of them lift up your shirt and the other half bite you."

"Stucco!" he told me on the walk back up the bluff. "I'm telling you, stucco is the way to go up here with all these trees and everything. It's like, unexpected—it goes against the grain."

"Nobody up here builds in stucco," I told him and looked at Patricia, who appeared to be feeling as desperate as I was. "They don't do stucco."

"Do I care? I'm bringing in my own guys anyway. Mexicans. Nobody does stucco like Mexicans. You and I'll work it out so we can share a dish for cable and a huge freezer down at my place."

I stopped in the path and looked at him. "We don't even have public power here, Stanley—just a generator. And Patricia and I don't want cable."

He studied me. "Not now you don't have power. Not now you don't want cable. But I'm talking down the road, pal—when we get up here."

"Way down the road," said Linda.

"We can share a guest house, too. I'm thinking the Runt and some of the guys might like it up here—little getaway." Stanley clapped me on the back. "Hey. Challie. You don't want cable, you don't hook into the dish. See? Simple. But don't come over trying to watch the hockey games on mine."

At the top of the bluff we stopped again to look out over the bay and Stanley asked who owned the big, uninhabited island at the mouth of Tracadie Harbor. I told him I had no idea, probably a lot of people.

"We could buy it maybe, put up a marina. Where's the nearest marina?"

"I don't know. Baddeck, I guess. But I don't want to buy the island and put up a marina, Stanley—even if I had the money, which I don't."

"Neither does Stanley," said Linda, sighing. "Can we go inside now?"

"We can look into it. It's worth looking into, is all I'm saying," Stanley said.

Patricia and I were in a barely contained panic when we met Stanley and Linda for dinner that night at their motel. But Stanley brought to the table his sweet, funny, generous self; he was calm; he didn't mention satellite dishes, freezers, or Mexican builders. And Linda told Patricia in the ladies' room that it would be years before they could spend enough time in Nova Scotia to warrant building a house, and that she wasn't much taken with the bugs and the remoteness anyway. As far as she was concerned, their investment up here was totally passive and would stay that way.

On the ride back to the cabin Patricia and I decided not to worry any more over the host of fright-wig images the afternoon had conjured: limos full of movie people driving through East Tracadie on their way to the "guest house"; stucco buildings sprouting like mushrooms on the shores of Linwood Harbor; "the Runt" borrowing sugar at midnight; and, worst of all, the vision of arguments with Stanley over dozens of things it now seemed we were dead certain to argue over. We realized on the one hand that we had made a mistake, one that truly could jeopardize everything we were doing in Nova Scotia and that was almost certain to kill off a valued friendship; on the other hand, we realized there was nothing we could do now to rectify that mistake, other than to hope Linda was right.

I had promised to take Latham and Rob bass fishing, finally, the next day in the Annapolis valley. At dinner Stanley had turned down an invitation to join us, saying he would rather have a look around the area with Patricia and Linda.

When the boys and I got back from fishing the following night, Patricia was in bed reading, and Rob and Latham and I could feel her anger as soon as we stepped into the cabin. She looked at us over the top of her reading glasses. "Get a beer, sit down, and listen to this," she said.

Patricia is a woman with very few sharp angles. She is mostly soft curves and, mostly, life deflects off of her. One of her best friends, a self-described "crisp" woman, calls Patricia's particular and opposite quality "luscious." It is an apt word to describe her perfectly ripe sweetness, the fluency of her emotions, and her tropically languid momentum through life. People feel as absorbed and relaxed by Patricia as by the Gulf of Mexico. Meeting and being with her, in that way, is a tangible experience, as is the weight and sharpness of her intelligence in counterpoint to the give of her personality when you get to know her well. Patricia is luscious in a way that only small, happy, unflappable things can be, and it requires almost a lifetime's commitment to make her angry. But it can be done, and Stanley had done it.

After a perfectly nice morning, she said, he had asked Patricia to call Frank Chisholm, the real estate agent through whom we had bought our property, now a friend, and invite him up to the cabin for a chat. "He started off by telling Frank that we had all been screwed on the price of the seventy acres on

Linwood, but he was going to give Frank another chance. He said that you and he were interested in developing the island. Frank nearly dropped his tea. Stanley said, 'What would it take?' Frank said he had no idea. Then Stanley said, listen to this, 'I know this is sort of the sticks up here, but I'm from L.A., and I know about development. Now, if I thought you'd play it straight with me and Challie and not try to stick it to us like you did on the last deal . . .' That's when I blew up—I swear to God I wanted to carve his face off. I said, 'This is my house, goddamnit Stanley, and we built it with our own damn hands and we by God sweated over it and suffered over it. We're *homesteading* up here and . . .' "

Patricia was out of bed now, pinwheeling around the room in her nightgown, her reading glasses still on her nose. Latham and Rob watched her with their mouths open.

" '. . . we've made good friends, and this man is one of them, and I'll be goddamned if I'll have you insult him in my house.' Well, poor Stanley looked so horrified I got to feeling bad, so then I said, 'I'm sorry I shouted at you, Stanley. I'm going out to our tent for ten minutes to calm down.' When I came back he was gone."

"Jesus Christ," said Latham appreciatively.

"What did Frank do?" I asked.

"He left too." Patricia cocked her head and grinned. "He looked as horrified as Stanley did."

Stanley called the next morning at seven. Stiffly, he told me that he and Linda had decided to leave early—that day, in fact. They had a plane back to L.A. at noon. I asked them if Patricia and I could meet them in town for breakfast. Stanley cleared his throat. "Maybe Tricia'd rather not," he said quietly.

"She wants to," I said. "We'll meet you at your motel in thirty minutes."

"What's red and got seven little dents in it?" Stanley's voice was brighter.

"I don't know."

"Snow White's cherry . . . the Runt's gonna love it."

On the way into town neither of us talked much except to agree that we had no idea what to say to Stanley. But it didn't matter. Stanley knew what to say and he was magnificent. Staring at his corned beef hash, he said that he and Linda had decided that Nova Scotia was not for them. He hoped we'd understand. They would either keep their ownership in the land as an investment for as long as we liked, or we could buy them out, whenever we wanted, at exactly the price they had paid for it. No interest. Interest wasn't for good friends, and that's what we were, and he and Linda hoped we would always be.

Patricia and I both wanted to kiss him, and we did. Then we kissed Linda, who was clearly delighted with the way things had turned out, and we drove back out to our cabin. Not a word had been said about the meeting with Frank.

In the car Patricia was back off cock to her salubrious self, looking out the window, ready as ever to meet anything the world threw up with pliant aplomb. Part of the thrill of her company for nearly thirty years has been this serene, unqualified readiness. Her eagerness to collaborate on whatever came up, and her dislike of confrontation and strife, for years had made Patricia easy meat for various invaders. I had been one of those invaders, and she now viewed her old disinclination to fight with me until it was too late, even to protect herself, as her main contribution to the sabotage of our marriage. She was still ready for anything. But now, as she and Stanley had learned for the first time the day before, she would fight when invaded—and at the front door rather than the back.

"So you were really fierce yesterday?" I said, sorry I had missed the show with Stanley and Frank.

She stared out the window and didn't answer for a while. "You would have been too. I felt like I was defending us—our whole life now. But not so much against Stanley. Stanley is nothing but sweet, and he didn't mean any harm. Against our old life, I think—what we used to be."

She stared out the window still, and I couldn't see her wide blue eyes, but I knew them, and I knew they were happy. I thought about the miracle of those eyes seeing with mine a new life in a chunk of wild, northern land. Love for grown-up people is about lives growing to fit each other in the real world; everything else is just dinner music.

We were all glad—Patricia and I, Latham and Rob—to have twelve days left to ourselves alone in Nova Scotia after Stanley and Linda left, and to be able to use those days to add a few whimsical or lazy flourishes to the sturdy, practical summer we had built.

Just before Stanley and Linda had arrived, Tom Mattie had cleared five acres of land in front of the cabin and started bulldozing a pond for us out of a little marshy area near the cabin; by the time they left, we had a muddy, half-acre hole in the ground, six to eight feet deep, that was filling slowly with springwater. Tom had left a little grassy island in the middle for ducks to nest on and had carved the pond into a pretty bell shape around the island—making more, as usual, out of a job than you could imagine for it. Fields immediately understood this pond to be his. He trotted down to it for a swim first thing every morning and revisited it four or five times during the day. On a number of evenings he and I sat shoulder to shoulder in the rushes at the pond's south end as if we were in a blind waiting for ducks. Fields would stare at the distant gulls and crows with his ears cocked forward and his brow furrowed, and I would put on my game face too and practice following the flight of a hawk or a gull with just my eyes, with no head movement to give us away.

The weather went dead calm and well into the nineties for three days running. Dog days, Edna Boudreau called them, fanning herself on our deck. They often got a few of them in August, she said, and they caused strange things to happen.

"I miss being out on the water now that Walter doesn't have a boat," she said, fanning and looking out at the bay, which was as hot and bright and motionless as a blue car hood baking in the sun. "If something strange is going to happen, you might as well be out on the water for it."

So we tied the dogs in the shade, left them a bowl of water, and took Edna mackerel fishing in the boat. While we trolled, she sat in the stern, smiling and cool now, watching the coastline she had lived on all her life.

When we got back to the cabin Arthur was sick. He had been low on energy and appetite for a few days, and I had been watching him. That afternoon when I untied him he followed me off the blueberry shack's deck with one of his hind legs dragging. He couldn't stand at all on that leg and the other hind leg was weak. Latham and Rob and I watched him for a while, then drove him into the vet's office in Antigonish. The vet had no idea what was wrong, he said, but he would keep Arthur overnight and give him some tests.

The next day was the hottest yet, topping ninety degrees before noon, without a stir of air. Fields and I went down to the pond early. I sat on a broiled clump of mud, and Fields took a swim. He trotted over to shake muddy water on me, then lay down and propped his head on my leg to study the pond. It was absolutely still and warming fast under the climbing sun. This day's god was going to be another bully, the sun in his hand like a red whip, running everything into hiding.

Fields and I went back to the cabin for breakfast and I called the vet. He said Arthur couldn't stand now on either of his back legs. He would run the tests today and should know something by that evening.

Latham and Rob spent the morning and part of the afternoon building an insulated house for the generator. They built it out of heavy plywood, put vents in it, hinged a door to it, and covered it with a blue-tin roof. I went back and forth from watching and lazily helping them to helping Patricia sow the vegetable garden with buckwheat. Around five o'clock she and I decided to walk down to the beach with Fields for a swim. But out at the end of the cape my hips began to ache from trudging through the heat, and I turned around. Fields wanted to go with Patricia, but I made him come with me. He had been drinking saltwater at the beach whenever he was hot, and I had a vague sense that that wasn't good for him, so I called him away from Patricia and we headed back for the cabin. After a while I saw Fields's tail begin to windmill, its pale blonde underfeathers catching light, and he dove into the brush after a scent. I kept walking.

Thirty yards up the trail, when Fields hadn't reappeared,

I stopped and called him. He didn't come, so I stood there and called again. A bright, disquieting stillness, thin and sharp as a knife blade, fell across the cape on these dog day afternoons. There was a shrill, silvery pitch to the light, like a reflection off of chrome. A warbler back in the spruces was building a floor and four struts on the air—laying down a long, level, low note, then nailing four corner-post notes quickly into it. At certain times this song sounded like the air itself; in that hot glare it was like a form of craziness. I called Fields again. He didn't come. I limped back to the cabin.

About a half hour later Patricia had returned and I decided to drive down to the beaver pond for a swim. I walked outside and called Fields. Rob shouted to me that he was under the deck, one of his favorite places, and acting strangely. In fact, he was dying of heatstroke. Rob and Latham and I pulled him out from under the deck where he had been trying to dig and eat himself into the earth. His mouth was foaming and full of dirt. I shouted to Patricia to get the truck and Rob and Latham and I picked him up and laid him in the back. Fields couldn't control his beautiful head and his body was beginning to convulse. We rushed him down to the pond and carried him into it. Latham held him in the shallow, muddy water and I tried to throw water down his throat. He was convulsing. I got my hand stuck in his mouth and felt his jaws reflexively closing on it. Somehow he threw off the convulsion and gently let my hand go before even the skin was broken. Then he stretched out in Latham's arms, shivered, and died.

Patricia and Rob stood on the bank. Latham and I kneeled in the water. Latham hugged Fields to his chest and face. Their blond hair mingled in the pond. I looked up at Patricia and

Rob. Both of their faces were vague and blurry with shock. Like all instants of sudden, unthinkable loss, this moment seemed impossible and way beyond words.

"He made it home before he died," I said finally. "Thank God for that." I could have said that he had died in the arms of the human being, who, along with me, loved him best, and thanked God for that also. But I could not have said what seemed truer than anything else right then—that a part of me felt absolutely and irreparably ruined.

Fields was just a dog, of course, but for a while a few years before he had been closer to me than any person. He was always closer to me than any dog had been, except for maybe his father. And no dog has ever been just a dog to me. Too, like all the other lives up there that summer, Fields's joyful life was mine to take care of, and for that afternoon, I hadn't; I had let the jeopardy catch us.

And it wasn't through with us yet. When Rob, Latham, and I drove Fields's body in to the vet that night to have an autopsy done, he told us Arthur was very sick with something he couldn't identify, and getting worse. For a diagnosis we would have to take him to a veterinary hospital on Prince Edward Island.

The next morning we picked up Fields's body and buried it beside the new pond. The vet told us he had died from a massive heatstroke that had left his internal temperature over 110 degrees three hours after he died. Drinking seawater all summer, he said, would have dehydrated Fields, making him a sitting duck for heatstroke. Then we picked up Arthur, drove to Pictou, and took the ferry over to Prince Edward Island.

On the three-hour ferry ride to the island, Latham wandered around putting his purple-lensed sunglasses on various people aboard the boat and taking photographs of them for what he told them was a book he was doing on people on ferries wearing the same pair of purple-lensed sunglasses. Then, back in the car, I saw this gentle, oblique, ardent-hearted son of ours crying soundlessly behind those sunglasses as we pulled out of the belly of the ship.

Patricia sat in the restaurant of the ferry for the entire trip and read through twelve magazines, moving her lips, without looking up. Rob sat with her, staring at his hands. And I walked around for a while, then stood on the boat's rear deck looking into the Northumberland Strait for a sign of bluefin tuna and thought once that events roll up in time like a boat's garbage in the prop wash, making our day or breaking our hearts, then sinking again.

Arthur, it turned out, had cancer of the spine. An operation didn't help and almost killed him. The vet at the hospital called me on August 22, the day before we left Nova Scotia for the summer. He had come to be fond of Arthur and to admire the way that dignified animal bore his pain and spreading paralysis. We had three options, the vet said: another operation that would almost certainly kill the dog; taking Arthur home for the two or three months he might live, with a sort of cart for him to drag himself around on; or putting him to sleep. It was clear what the vet felt we should do, and after a half hour on the phone of trying to find a way around it, I told him to go ahead and do it.

It was fine all that last day in Nova Scotia. It was a day Arthur and Fields would have loved, with fall and woodcock on the air. We boarded up all the windows of the cabin with plywood, stored the generator, and turned off the water and the gas. At exactly eight o'clock there was a magnificent sunset, the last for us of many over the summer. Latham, Rob, and Patricia and I watched from the deck until the sky faded and there was just the winking of the green light at the mouth of Tracadie Harbor. Then we went inside and spent the next few hours in candlelight, visiting with nearly a dozen people who came up to our new home to tell us good-bye.

8

Michel Boudrot, born in 1601, emigrated to Port Royal in Acadia from his home at La Rochelle, France, in 1642. That this first Boudrot in Nova Scotia was an educated man can be assumed from the fact that he was soon appointed king's counsellor, lieutenant general, and judge in the hard little seaport of Port Royal on the Bay of Fundy.

Michel's great-grandson, Charles, born in 1714, fled Port Royal with his family to Windsor, Nova Scotia, before the British expulsion of the Acadians in 1755. Other less farsighted Boudrots, who stayed in Port Royal, were exiled to New York, Maryland, Georgia, and elsewhere. Some were returned to France. Some found their way to Louisiana.

Charles and his family were jailed briefly in Halifax by the British. Upon their release they joined a small group of other Acadian escapees from the expulsion who had settled in the village of Chezzetcook on the eastern shore of Nova Scotia. Charles's oldest son, Jean, married his second cousin in Chezzetcook in 1775; their first son, Hilarion, married a woman named Marie Deslauriers, changed the spelling of his surname to Boudreau, and moved his family in the early 1800s to the settlement of East Tracadie on Saint Georges Bay.

East Tracadie and its sister village, Tracadie, sit on opposite sides of Tracadie Harbor. Archeological evidence indicates that Micmac Indians and their progenitors occupied the shoreline and islands of this lovely, bountiful harbor in large numbers from as early as twenty-five hundred to three thousand years ago, making it one of the oldest Indian settlements in Nova Scotia. Indians were never fools about places to live: The area around Tracadie and its harbor was popular with them because of good weather, protection from storms, and an abundance of game, fresh water, fish, and shellfish.

These same virtues were immediately apparent to one Pierre Benoit when he happened onto Tracadie Harbor in 1776 and became the first white man to settle there, in a log cabin he built for himself on the harbor's eastern shore. Benoit was a good friend of the Micmacs. He spoke their language and was held in high esteem by them. And he served as an interpreter of language and custom between the Micmacs and the other Acadians who began shortly to settle around East Tracadie, making that settling as pleasant and fruitful as the area itself. Like Benoit, these Acadians were among the few who were wily or lucky enough to have avoided the expulsion. By 1787 there were twelve families of them, including Benoit's, in the Tracadie area, and in that year Lieutenant Governor Parr of Nova Scotia ordered a surveyed thirty-six hundred acres to be divided among them.

One of these families was that of a French mariner named Joseph Barrio. The three hundred or so acres he was granted were on the east side of the harbor, overlooking its mouth and reaching north into Saint Georges Bay in a high, dramatic headland, or cape, that came to be known as Barrio's Head. When Hilarion Boudreau's family moved to East Tracadie around 1800, Joseph Barrio married one of Hilarion's daughters. When Hilarion and his wife died, the youngest of their twelve children, Simon, was adopted by Joseph Barrio and his wife, and after their deaths, Simon became the first Boudreau to own Barrio's Head.

The Acadians were not the only settlers to end a flight of exile in and around Tracadie in search of a new start, a piece of land, and peace. Also in 1787 Lieutenant Governor Parr granted three thousand acres in Tracadie to seventy-four petitioners for farmland from a nearby community of Black Loyalists, both freemen and slaves, who had fled America after the Revolution. And in 1825 a French monk named Father Vincent De Paul Merle and a few companions founded and built, a couple of miles south of Tracadie Harbor, the first Trappist monastery in North America. The monastery was called Le Petit Clairvaux. Its monks were dedicated to the spiritual care of the Indian, Acadian, and black inhabitants of the Tracadie area, as well as to their own prayer and penance. They operated saw- and gristmills and farmed the land around the monastery—making do in much the same way as everyone else did.

From the first Acadian presence there, work in East Tracadie meant family work. Acadian families, like Micmac families, had to be close and virtually self-sufficient in order to survive. Throughout the nineteenth century and much of the twentieth, life was lived mostly on small farms. Large families spread the work around and allowed the men to fish or do something else to supplement the living. The family work on those small farms was constant. There was always clearing land and building fences. There were cows, horses, sheep, pigs, and hens to take care of, firewood to cut and haul, and logs to cut and saw for repairs and additions; there was plowing in the spring and fall, planting, harvesting, and haymaking; cattle hides were tanned with hemlock bark, rubbed with dogfish oil, and made into harness and shoe leather, horse reins, laces, and skate straps; linen was made from flax; sheep's wool was sheared, washed, carded, and spun, died with moss, onion skin, and barks, and then knitted or woven into clothing; cherries, berries, and vegetables were preserved for the winter; sarsaparilla, chokecherries, and elderberries were picked for wine, and hazelnuts were picked and ripened in the haymow for Christmas; seabird nests were raided in the spring for eggs; partridge, ducks, rabbits, 'coon, deer, moose, and bear were hunted; and there was always fishing to do in the harbor and bay for herring, mackerel, cod, salmon, flounder, mussels, and clams, and through the ice in winter for eel, smelt, and sea trout.

As soon as a child could walk he was taught to pick berries, or potato bugs, or rocks out of a field. Before going to school in the morning a daughter would bring the cows in from pasture and milk them, feed the pigs and hens, cut kindling, and draw water; then she would do those same things again after school.

The smallest boy could put rocks in the lobster pots as "loose ballast" to help sink the traps until they were water-soaked. As he got older he could put mackerel on the spindles for bait.

In a few years he could carry the traps to be loaded onto the boat and pass them down to his older brother, who would pack the load.

In a few more years he could be on the boat himself, accepting the traps from a younger brother and packing them according to his father's instructions.

And a few years after that he could take over the boat from his father, who would replace Grandpa on the shore mending traps and teaching the youngsters how to bait them and put in rocks for loose ballast.

Now in East Tracadie, family work goes on much as it has since 1787. So does Sunday Mass in the family pew. So do nightly family card games, parties on the beach, and packed wedding-reception dances at the parish hall, where fiddlers and players of harmonicas, accordions, and guitars get great-grand-parents to toddlers square and step dancing.

There are some forty families now in East Tracadie and practically all of them are related. There are thirteen heads of households named Boudreau, most of whom are related to the DeCostes, of whom there are eight heads of households. There are three Cotie families, two Bonvies, two Deloreys, etc. Over 20 percent of the men in the village work as fishermen; over 25 percent are or have been farmers. These two traditional and primary industries of the area are both in serious decline, as is the Canadian National Railroad that had employed 10 percent of East Tracadie's men.

With around 50 percent of the villagers' jobs in either immediate or long-term danger, with a chronically recessed economy and with the various lures of city life just a few miles down the road in Truro, Sydney, or Halifax, East Tracadie is now an easy place to leave, particularly for the young. And yet very few of its citizens, young or old, do leave. Families don't break up. On a summer afternoon you can see them making hay, families and neighbors together. And in the evening of that same day you can see them playing volleyball after the haying is done, the same families and neighbors together in someone's backyard on opposite sides of an old, frayed net.

It is increasingly difficult for many of these families to keep land that can no longer be worked for enough profit or provision to make a living. That land in many cases came down to them from one of Lieutenant Governor Parr's original grants. A generation ago owning land in East Tracadie was an unquestioned birthright, a priceless heritage of independent subsistence living. A generation from now, many of East Tracadie's citizens realize, a Boudreau, a Pettipas, a Cotie, or a DeCoste might be lucky to own five acres, down some two hundred from what his original forebear here was granted. And if East Tracadie is ever really discovered by developers, this business of land will certainly get more complicated.

For the time being the families of East Tracadie hold on to what they can, stay together, and stay put. Like the Mi'kmaq who lived here before them, the Acadians of East Tracadie are family people accustomed to making do with what they have. And, whatever they may have lost, what they still have in East Tracadie, the thing that holds them here and defeats all the forces nudging them out, is a homeplace—a still warm and glowing hearth.

The homeplace to an Acadian Nova Scotian is what the Cape Breton writer Clive Doucet calls "the village of my father and his father . . . a hometown of the mind and heart" whose real streets are the continuity of memory. The homeplace is a living symbol of continuity and safety in the face of outmigration and social fragmentation, a place of helping and loving, and of knowing—knowing your neighbors, your trade, your land, your genealogy, the weather, and what it is you don't care to know. In East Tracadie and other homeplaces in Nova Scotia people keep the ancient recipes to rappie pie, pollen pancakes, steamed fiddleheads, dandelion beer, and *gaspereau* boiled in vinegar. The old people aren't let go of into nursing homes, but kept around to step dance, play the fiddle, tell stories, and provide wisdom. The young people aren't let go of either, but build their homes within a winter's walk of the homes of their parents and grandparents. And throughout the day the local radio station announces birthdays, anniversaries, and weddings as if those things were news, and notes births and deaths to keep the community up on its familial comings and goings.

The original Acadian communities in Nova Scotia along the Bay of Fundy were small and isolated, spread out along the banks of inlets and brackish rivers, where there were marshes that could be diked and turned into farmland. The people in each of these communities were absolutely on their own and absolutely dependent on mutual cooperation in the construction and maintenance of the dikes that afforded them a living. Now as then, homeplace to an Acadian is, finally, where life is as isolated from the bigger world and as interdependent as life within a family—where everyone's fingers are in the same dike.

The piece of land known as Barrio's Head in East Tracadie was passed along from Simon Boudreau to his son Joseph, and then from Joseph to his three sons, Walter, Anthony, and Ernest. Walter Boudreau married his second cousin, just as his great-great-grandfather Jean had, and that woman, Edna Boudreau, also had a family interest in Barrio's Head.

Barrio's Head had originally been in hardwood. In 1829 a fire started in Bayfield, jumped Tracadie Harbor, and burned to Havre Boucher, destroying every tree on the peninsula. The land was cleared of its dead trees and fenced, and for 142 years it was used as pasture for cattle, horses, and sheep. At one point shortly after the fire, local soldiers trained on it for a war that never happened.

Edna Boudreau remembers herding in cows from Barrio's Head to a corral for milking before she walked to school in the mornings, and then again in the evenings after school—on a stormy evening the cows might have been all the way over at Linwood Harbor. In 1972 she and Walter got rid of the last of their cattle and sheep, and they and Edna's brother Calvin began raising blueberries on the land. At picking time in the fall they had big parties up on the cape—barbecues and corn-and-lobster boils—and Edna would make blueberry pies and muffins and steamed blueberry puddings for the people who came up to help with the back-torturing work of raking berries. One year Edna picked a ton of berries herself between her regular chores of keeping house and cooking for Walter and the other pickers. Their biggest harvest was nine tons one year, and they also picked a ton of cranberries that fall. They would drive their berries into East River, Saint Mary's, to sell in the evenings. One night they were given a check for eight hundred dollars for two days' picking and they felt like they were millionaires. But what pleased them most was that everyone always told them that Barrio's Head berries were the best and sweetest they had ever eaten.

In the mid-1980s the blueberries got to be too much work and Walter, Edna, and Calvin stopped harvesting them. Barrio's Head sat there, unused, going back to brush and scrub. In 1991 Edna and Walter and his brothers needed money and they decided to sell Barrio's Head. My family bought it. We were the first people not named Barrio or Boudreau to own it; we were the first people neither Acadian nor Micmac to occupy it; and we were the first people ever to build a home on it.

Childless and dogless, Patricia and I returned to that home for the first few weeks of October to try out living in it by ourselves. We hadn't known how we would feel returning to the cabin alone, but when we drove up the shale road and first saw the cabin, looking like a small, sturdy ship in a new green sea of hay, we both could have yelped with joy over being back.

Walter's and Edna's grandson Shawn had turned on the water and gas for us, set up the generator, and taken the plywood shutters off the windows. And Nicole Andrews had come up and cleaned the inside of the cabin, stocked it with food, and put kindling and logs in the wood box. Patricia and I walked into the spotless, well-supplied cabin with nothing to do but start living in it.

The pond that Fields had died in was now almost bankfull. The five cleared acres around the cabin that had been red mud when we left in August were now ankle-high in a mixture of hay and oats so freshly green that in late afternoon light it looked fluorescent. The weather was magnificent, wood-stove cold at night and in the early mornings, and warming usually into the seventies during the day. Most days were clear and calm with clarion blue skies and a few cotton-ball clouds to sail shadows over the bay.

Out on the cape the brush had gone from green to a vivid, purplish red. The hardwood stands among the spruces were crimson and yellow. With no dogs to chase them off, our resident wild animals were much more forthcoming. Deer grazed almost every evening along the seam between the new hay and the brush, and tracks showed them coming down to the pond at night to drink. The cleared land was full of rabbits during the day. A lethargic old porcupine visited too, walking with a stiff-hipped waddle much like my own, to chew content-edly on spears of oats. And more than once we saw coyotes at the back edge of the hay near the pond. There was one big male in particular: He would come trotting out of the brush with that beautiful masculine way of carrying real, effective weight lightly—up on the toes—that so many athletes have, and ghost across the green hay grinning, then slide into the brush again.

There is often a garden in restarted relationships, much like a childhood garden, where the landscape seems en-chanted—where the air is sweeter, the colors brighter, and the mornings more fragrant and stirring than they have ever been. Those two weeks in October were that garden for Patricia and me. Over the past summer we had planted it and walled it in, and now it was fully in bloom.

We discovered that there were squirrels living in our insulation, and that the French doors leaked in a strong north wind, as did the joint between the cabin and shed roofs in a good south wind. And when the wind was out of the east, the water heater's pilot light blew out. In terms of living space and simplicity of living conditions, we had come full circle to living again as we had in Ireland. And we were both delighted with that. I would get up early to start the wood stove, make coffee, read, and watch for coyotes in the hay. After breakfast I wrote, sometimes on the bluff, and Patricia painted or read or made dried arrangements out of branches of berries and crab apples and milkweed pods. In the afternoons we would walk the beach to Linwood Harbor, or go down to Barrio's Beach, where she would set up an easel and paint on the shore while I kayaked in the bay. We rode mountain bikes out along the deserted Cape Jack road and clammed in Linwood Harbor.

One day there we came up on Bill the Rambler, rambling the beach, his spirit and snaggletoothed old grin as bright as ever. He had missed us, he said. We asked him how he would spend the winter and he said he just happened to have an idea on that. There was a protected little apple orchard on our property in the harbor. The Rambler said he might be willing to park his trailer up on blocks there for the winter. It was a nice spot, no north wind, not a long snowshoe into town. And he could guard our eastern flank down there against vandals and them damned snowmobilers, the old knife-thrower said.

Patricia smiled and told him it would be a great favor to us if he would do that.

The Rambler reached into his jacket pocket and pulled out a new white teacup with blue forget-me-nots around the inside of its lip and gold block script around the outside that read: ONE FRIEND LIKE YOU IS ALL ANYONE NEEDS. Bill handed the cup to Patricia with a barely noticeable bow.

"I bought this for you in the summer, and I've carried it around all fall," he said.

Patricia kissed him carefully on the cheek and put the cup into the mesh bag she carried to bring back to the cabin whatever she found interesting.

"You're a lucky man," Bill told me gravely.

"I know that," I said. Then he turned with a little salute and rambled off down the beach.

I went salmon fishing a couple of times with our friend

Dave Clark, the telephone lineman and ace salmon angler, who kindly introduced me to some pools he had known so long and well they were like relatives. Otherwise I didn't leave the cabin without Patricia. For the first autumn in over twenty-five years I had no urge at all to hunt birds.

Patricia and I had worried that we might find it lonely at the cabin without dogs or family. The day after we arrived she spent the afternoon at the DeCostes' house bathing and feeding baby Sam and talking to Jake about tractors, his favorite topic. She took a number of long walks with the two DeCoste girls and with Amanda and Nicole Andrews. Nicole, who was a sophomore at the college in Antigonish, came up to see us every day, as did Reggie Beshong. Tommy and Mary Mattie came for a visit several times. So did Walter and Edna Boudreau, and we had supper at their house one night. Andy and Heather DeCoste came by, and big Glenn Bears, and Ron and Sue McNeil. And we saw Maria and Ralph DeCoste almost every day.

But even had we not seen a single neighbor or friend during that time, Patricia and I would not have felt for a second lonely. We were then exactly at the right point, precisely old enough as a couple and as individuals, to realize that every single thing you do in life counts and is indelible. Living on that premise day to day in our little house was like sitting on a fence together talking through the afternoon and then wondering where the time went. It felt richly autonomous and as obscurely unfair as playing Ravel's *Concerto for the Left Hand* with both hands.

My wife and I were in love again, as passionately as when we were in our twenties, but with a new self-reliance that would have been impossible then and that was at least partially a gift of the past summer. As much as we missed our children at the cabin, Patricia and I found with some surprise that we didn't need them there. And we realized that part, out of much, of what the summer and the place had given us was a peace made with where we were in life and a sense of permanent sufficiency in each other. We had done over the summer what we had most wanted to do—reclaimed at least for a while our family intimacy. And, in the cabin alone, Patricia and I found that we had reclaimed each other as well.

During the time she and I were separated I had dreamed about a simple, self-delighting life with her on the other side of that separation, and that was precisely the life we lived at the cabin in October. I had dreamed of flannel shirts, and we wore them; of thick soups, and we made and ate them. Back in the misery of our separation there was a dreamed-of joy in her company— particularly a wordless company while we worked or read in some snug, small place, the air between us thick with reassurances—and I had that joy every day at the cabin in October. There had been back then a dreamed-of bliss at seeing her happily engaged at something from a distance, and I recognized that bliss in déjà vu from my kayak one day in October when I came around a point and saw her painting on the beach. I had dreamed while we were separated of making love in the woods again, as we used to do in New Hampshire in the autumn, and of playing board games late at night while moths tapped on a screen—and in October at the cabin we did those things. And when we were separated I had dreamed of our being the complete focus of each other's attention again, as we had been when we were first married, and at the cabin in October we were that.

Nothing makes time as valuable as concentration to the point of empathy. With our attentions buried in each other deep enough to feel even the slightest stirrings, Patricia and I felt like moguls of time at our cabin in October. We had long conversations day and night, but we could also work all a rainy day together by the stove without speaking a word and end the day feeling full of each other. And every sunset watched together, every meal cooked or trip taken to town together, was a hit jackpot. We felt overwhelmingly complete and prepotent in each other's company—as if we needed nothing more than that company to found the city of Rome or fly to the moon.

Alone together at our cabin in October, Patricia and I caught an abundant grace of renewal as easily as you fill a tin cup in a rainstorm. And we came to feel like virtuosos of our own old dreams, getting better and sweeter music from them than we had ever thought possible.

One night (after some Oriental food in Antigonish), I dreamed I was standing on the beach in the dark, a small surf hissing in the pebbles at my feet. It was stormy, and as I stood there I could see bright, horizontal, elliptical seams of thunder in the sky. Out on the sea, separated from me by maybe a mile of black water, was a big ship, all lit up and festive looking. I had no idea where the ship was going or who was on it, but I knew without doubt that the only future I had was on board that ship. I also knew that there were all kinds of things in the mile or so of dark water that could kill or wound me before I reached the ship, and I had the sense that many people had tried and failed to reach it—that the bottom of the sea here was strewn with failed swimmers. But there wasn't any choice of what to do, so I walked into the sea and started swimming for the ship.

When I awoke from this dream it was just dawn on a Sunday. I rolled out of bed with the bright ship still in my mind, feeling the dread of the swim, and limped over to start the woodstove. Wadding up newspaper, I looked out the French doors and saw the big male coyote standing still at the far edge of the hay field above the pond. It was another beautiful morning, with the sun just up over Linwood Harbor and a few fishing boats already well out on the bay, leaving smooth wakes on the calm sea. The coyote was staring at the ground. It was the first time I had ever seen a coyote standing still, and I wanted a look at him unobstructed by the mullions in the French doors. I went out the back door of the cabin, hobbling from the early morning stiffness in my hips. I crouched up to the deck at the front of the cabin and lifted my head just high enough to look across the deck at the coyote. He was still there, still standing still, the ruff of fur on top of his neck and his long, upright ears backlit and silvered by the rising sun. Father coyote—to some American Indians his devotion to mate and cubs made him the animal kingdom's symbol of the family man, a *tête de la maison* with teeth. This one pounced suddenly, and a rabbit spurted out from between his paws and disappeared into the brush with the coyote zagging behind it like a quarter horse.

I stood up straight and stretched, feeling suddenly wonderful, even happy with my dream. If I could no longer run, and barely walk, that was all right, since there was no place I really wanted to go. And I could still swim—even for a mile in the dark if I had to.

I went back into the cabin to make coffee—and decided to build a big breakfast for Patricia and me. While I cooked and Patricia snoozed, I put some Strauss on our boom box for early morning entertainment and cranked it up—the waltzes, music that carried images with it into that cabin with no TV. Nine-teenth-century court Austrians in brocaded jackets and gowns winked at each other as I fried the sausage, ran to the outbuild-ings of the palace with billets-doux as I made the toast, and waltzed across waxed floors to that great, lovely musical chitchat, those majestic, sentimental string crescendos that must have gathered whole ballrooms up into the sense that anything was worth giving up for the partner you were dancing with, for the unwashed, scented ear you were whispering into.

When everything was cooked but the eggs, I whipped those with some fresh chives, left them standing on the stove, and retired to the bed for a waltz of my own—a family man making do.

That afternoon Patricia and I took a long bike ride (some-thing else, along with swimming and bed waltzing, I could still do) out to Cape Jack. Coming back we passed Ron and Sue McNeil's farm across from the fishing wharf, and Ron was outside playing volleyball with his kids and some of the De-Costes'. He had been plowing for winter wheat when we began our ride and was still in his overalls. As Patricia and I pedaled by he was throwing the ball up to serve, but he let it drop to wave to us, and all the kids turned around and waved too. A splash of yellow light was on them, and they squinted into it and waved. The jonquil-yellow light across the group seemed to freeze them into an image from some happily remembered dream.

In 1989, when Patricia and I came back together, we realized that we had both been dreaming for years of living in an unchic, unimpatient place with old, durable values and big, close families of people who look after and care for each other and pay attention to the things that matter; a solid, rooted place with a safe harbor, where people will stop a game or work to wave at neighbors. Nearly three years later, there was no question we had found all that in an old Micmac and Acadian homeplace.

There is an euphonious Spanish word for the area of a bullring where a bull, in its ordeal, comes to feel safest and bravest—the place to which he returns over and over again to face whatever comes next, including, finally, the sword. How a bull chooses such a place is certainly no more mysterious than how human beings do it. But however it was done, East Tracadie and Barrio's Head had come to be our *querencia*—the place in the ring where Patricia and I felt safest and boldest. We would go back to New Hampshire for the winter, but we would live here again next summer, we knew that—and next fall. And our children would come back here whenever they could; we knew that too. Next summer, if we could afford it, we would build a studio for Patricia and a writing shack for me, and maybe put in a road down to the harbor and a septic system for the cabin. We had already put our house in New Hampshire up for sale, and when we sold it we would build a bigger house out on the cape—the big Adirondack-style common building we had taken from *Your Cabin in the Woods*—and build more cabins around it for family and friends, and maybe even, someday, for use as a summer camp for underprivileged city kids. Running such a camp had been a dream of mine for a number of years, and Barrio's Head was made for it. Patricia and I would go back to New Hampshire the following day for the winter, but it was from this *querencia* that we would begin facing whatever came next.

We biked on past the McNeils' farm and Ralph and Maria DeCoste's house, past the wharf, and then out past Walter and Edna Boudreau's house to where the road ended at Barrio Beach and the entrance to Tracadie Harbor. We took the old, caving-in dirt road that ran east along the beach for a half a mile then steeply uphill over a little bluff and down along the beach again to the DeCostes' shack, where we and the kids and the dogs had spent our first nights of the summer. The sun was only a few minutes from setting, so Patricia and I hurried on up the shale road and out to the end of the cape to watch it. Out there at the end of Barrio's Head the air was hazel and cool, and two lines of black ducks scribed the sky over Cape Jack. We got off our bikes and sat on the tent platform Tom Mattie had dragged out for us in the summer. We looked down over the view to the west—Tracadie Harbor and Tracadie, Delorey Island and Bayfield—with its dreamlike, Arcadian plenitude, its promise of containing everything you could ever need. Out along Cape George there was a ridge of clouds, separated from the long peninsula by a band of clear sky. A few minutes before at the DeCostes' shack the sun had been behind that ridge, its light spilling from under it over the middle of the peninsula and then falling into the bay as an oval pool, a pot of gold, too bright to look at directly. Now as the sun sank below the clouds and into the band of clear sky, the gold pool of light ran across the bay—we could watch it come—and landed full on us. For a minute or two before it disappeared the sun hovered over Cape George, throwing a brilliant path directly across the bay to Patricia and me, and dropping its pot of gold smack onto old Joseph Barrio's Head.

✳   ✳   ✳

The day before we left Nova Scotia was Canadian Thanksgiving, and Ralph and Maria DeCoste invited us down to their house for Thanksgiving dinner. I smoked a big turkey on our smoker and we took it down to their house around four in the afternoon. It was a cloudy, wintry afternoon, the fifteenth of October. Patricia and I laid our coats on the bench in the entry hall, under a little framed piece of petit point that read, "Love is pulling together against all odds." It was the DeCoste family motto, and they practiced it. Five of the six children ran up and hugged us before we could make it into the kitchen. Over the summer and the past two weeks, Patricia and I had gotten closer to these kids (Jessica, 12, Chelsa, 11, Joshua, 9, Luke, 7, Jake, 4, and their one-year-old brother, Sam) than any since our own, and we were just as proud of them and delighted by them as grandparents.

In the kitchen Ralph poured some wine and we took it into the parlor to sit by the wood stove's hearth. Sam crawled up to Patricia and stuck up an arm to say he wanted her to pick him up. The old house smelled wonderfully of cooking vegetables and stuffing. The parlor was pleasantly warm, and the kids whirled in and out of it, bringing us new toys and pictures they had drawn. Maria sat on the couch with her wine, wearing her fine, ironic sense of humor on her face, and telling us about a wedding reception that she and Ralph had helped keep going until three o'clock that morning. Maria loves a party, as does Ralph, and both of them have a major talent for improvising fun in any company and for any occasion. Patricia and I and the rest of our crew had been the beneficiaries of many good times with them, and much kindness as well. They had opened their house and their family to us from the day we arrived. Ralph had given me a road right-of-way he hadn't had to give and had sold me a little piece of land that I needed and that he hadn't wanted to sell. They had brought us food, taken us to parties, and helped us throw rocks out of our vegetable garden. In no place we had ever lived had Patricia and I known neighbors as generous as these DeCostes, and over the course of just a few months they had become friends as valued as any we have.

Ralph refilled the wine glasses, set up a music stand, and began to fiddle, his smart, quick-to-grin Gallic face cocked on the instrument and bobbing to the music. The house we were sitting in had come down to Ralph from his grandfather. That grandfather was named Stephen Fougere. Stephen's wife, Ralph's grandmother, was Ida Boudreau, a sister of Walter's and a granddaughter of Simon Boudreau, the third owner of Barrio's Head. The land that Ralph's shack sat on, inherited from his grandmother, was originally part of the land we now owned.

Ralph was born in East Tracadie in the mid-fifties, in the same year his parents got indoor plumbing. He was one of nine children. His father was a fisherman who had farmed twenty acres; fishing and farming had provided everything the family needed to eat except for sugar, tea, macaroni, and peanut butter. As soon as he was old enough to know he would get older, Ralph wanted to get out of East Tracadie to see some of the rest of the world. And he did. He went off to school in Sydney to study chemistry. One summer he shipped to Greenland on a tramp freighter as helmsman and deckhand. When he finished school he took a job in Halifax at an oceanographic institute. He liked both the job and Halifax, but he found himself driving home to East Tracadie every other weekend. He went on oceanographic cruises in the Gulf of Saint Lawrence and to West Africa, and he found that he was like the Cape Breton coal miners who travel all over the world to work but never leave without a twig of spruce from the homeplace: Homeplace traveled with Ralph, too.

After a year in Halifax he was offered a job in Port Hawkesbury, and he took it because it was closer to East Tracadie. He met Maria in the town of Saint Peter's, where he was living while working in Port Hawkesbury. By then he had seen Montreal, New York, Paris, Chicago, and some of the countrysides of North America and Europe—enough of the world to know he didn't really need to see anymore. Maria was a nurse who had worked in Maine, and she didn't need to see anymore either. After a couple of months together they began to talk about half a dozen children and a farmhouse. There had been no question for a long time where Ralph wanted to go for that, so he and Maria got married and moved back to his grandfather's farmhouse in East Tracadie to get started on the half dozen kids. Ralph bought Maria a tractor for a wedding present.

Out of the forty-four heads of households in East Tracadie, Ralph DeCoste is the only one whose profession is listed as "computers." He has a late-twentieth-century job—setting up computers, teaching people how to use them, and writing computer programs—that won't dry up anytime soon into anachronism, as farming has done and fishing may soon for many of his neighbors. Ralph has a good trade, but there are plenty of places from which he could practice it on a faster track and for more money than from East Tracadie. He practices it from there because there he can live in his grandfather's house and bring his children up to put their fingers in the same dike that his are in.

We all ate Thanksgiving dinner squeezed in around the kitchen table, with Sam pulled up in his high chair. Ralph asked me to bless the food, and I did, and said truly to God that Patricia and I had much to be thankful for. After dinner there was more fiddle playing and Ralph brought out a bottle of grade-A moonshine. It was decided that Patricia and I would stay a little later than we had intended to stay. Since it was not only Thanksgiving but our last night in East Tracadie, we had all the occasion we needed to improvise some fun and see how long it lasted.

Maria filled up a big plastic container with turkey and stuffing for us to take with us in the car the next day. In the Acadian villages of Nova Scotia, when someone sends you home with a container full of food or brings you a pie or a pot of soup—as people constantly do in those villages—the tradition is to fill that container or pie plate or pot with something you've cooked yourself before you return it. We told Maria we would bring her container back to her. In June.

When it was time for the kids to go to bed Maria let Patricia and me take Jake upstairs. At the top of the stairs Jake turned right for a tear down the hall. I grabbed him from behind by the waist and steered him into his bedroom, where he could look out at most of the houses in East Tracadie and know everyone in the big, extended family behind those various walls. Jake doesn't know how not to speak to strangers, because there aren't any where he lives. And when he goes to sleep every night it is with the peace of familiarity that makes sleep dreamless.

We are the sum of all our new beginnings, the product of all the new lives we've begun and the places that have housed those lives.

"Bedtime, *Maneen*," I told Jake, and handed him the tractor he always took to bed.

"Bedtime *what?*" he said.

"*Maneen*—it means little man. A friend of ours used to call Latham that a long time ago."